TM

A PUMA POINT PRODUCTION LLC

SUBSIDIARY OF

Ed French

ARTIST LLC

Written, illustrated, and designed by
Edward Glen French
POB 300, Cotopaxi, Colorado 81223

JUST THE RIGHT SIZE FOR YOUR BACKPACK!

Additional copies available on amazon.com

The author makes no claims to guarantee your success.
Maps and advice are only starting points.

Where do YOU Elk HUNT?

Find your own
"secret, private"
elk hunting
spots in COLORADO
and other states !

Ed French

WOODSMASTER

From one of the author's paintings. Available at www.edfrench.fineaw.com

PRE SEASON SCOUTING

June, 2004 Ed found two bulls going **_down_** at 9:00 am. Using techniques in this book the author later shot a superb six point bull with a bow on public land in Colorado. He located the elk lower on the mountain two years later in the direction of a stream. Sure enough in the direction the bulls were headed a stream springs out of the side of a mountain ridge, a somewhat unusual phenomena. He felt that the bulls were headed down rather than up at that time of day for water as at that time of day elk would normally be moving **_up_** to beds.

Note; Scouting is best done in the summer, perhaps with family on a fishing or camping trip. One of the worst mistakes some hunters make is to invade good elk country two to three days before season, sight in their rifles, drive all over, hike, etc., etc. Elk are intelligent animals and do not care for human scent, and all the racket that people generate. Ignorance of this factor causes elk to simply move out of range usually several miles away, out of reach. If you don't have the time and resources to scout a few months or weeks ahead of season at least enter what you hope to be a good area in as quiet a manner as possible.

ABOUT THIS BOOK
THE BOOK IS JUST A GREAT STARTING POINT

The most common question I get about hunting is, "where do you hunt?" Thus the title of this book. By writing this I'm sharing with anyone how to find great spots but I have developed the attitude of not telling exactly where. Best to think this through ahead of time.

This is a how to book written by an ordinary elk hunter who like all hunters has had some extraordinary experiences. It is not written for literary critics. It is not polished by an editor. It is not, "politically correct". This is the book I wish I could have owned back in 1958. Good hunting. May God bless.

It is a handbook for hunters who may not be privileged to hunt on leases or ranches with a guide where it takes big dollars. I have been privileged to hunt in those conditions only a couple times. It is very different and I enjoyed it, but this is a handbook for those on a budget. For those who can't justify a second mortgage, want to have a great time and hopefully bring home some "trophies" and food for the freezer. It is a book for first time elk and deer hunters, for those who live out of state or in Colorado and those who are struggling to find a good place to hunt. It will also serve those who have hunted maybe for years without much success. It can also aid those who can hire a guide or be packed in, etc. The lessons here can be applied to other big game species in some instances or to other states with modifications in your thinking for other climates, conditions, and terrains.

A map section is printed in the back to help you start your search. I certainly wish such information had been available to me in the past. If reincarnation were a fact I'd come back and do it all over again with this book. There is a "secret" to finding elk on page 22.

ABOUT THE AUTHOR

Ed French shot his first bull elk opening morning October 1958. He was 17. His Dad took him as his guest with a rancher friend from McCoy, Colorado. In camp that year was a friend of his Dad who was a world champion skeet shooter and accomplished sportsman. The previous year this gentleman had shot a bull elk running at 600 yards and called the shot, a shot aiming uphill at about a 40 degree angle, "In the heart." Dad said, "Come on !" When they got to the bull the .270 had put the bullet IN THE HEART.

Ed had been hunting with his Dad for about four years by this time, (small game and just along for the hike). Ed had become proficient at varmint hunting with a 30-06 Enfield Dad had "sporterized." "The Meat Wagon" as it was affectionately dubbed is capable of five shot dime sized groups at 100 yards. Dad had shot a "box car load" of deer and elk with it. Dad was a mechanical genius, engineer and gunsmith and had put a choke on the rifle, something that years later became somewhat common. Ed bought the rifle from his Dad when he was nineteen.

When he has had the liberty to hunt "at home" in Colorado Ed has had a 50% success rate with rifle on elk on public lands. He has hunted in Colorado about 45 of the last 50 years. He has a "gift" for finding elk. On one occasion with a friend from Indiana he went out of the RV park about ten miles up towards the Collegiate Range northwest of Buena Vista. They stopped out in the flats, now covered with houses, on elk winter range. It was about 8 am June, 1989. Ed set up a scope and focused it on a spot about half way up an avalanche chute and told his friend, "Right there should be some elk." Looking through the scope, they were pleasantly surprised to see a herd of thirteen cows, calves, and a couple bulls. Ed is also a husband, dad, grandfather, retired Disney World Senior Artist (Fifteen years), pilot and Bible teacher, and inventor. He was a Boy Scout and missionary artist, (15 years).

Ed is an adventurer and has hiked considerably in Alaska , hunted in Texas, Wisconsin, Pennsylvania, North Dakota, Florida, etc. He has traveled in Hawaii and Venezuela. A passion of his is elk hunting with the bow in wilderness areas by backpack. He became proficient at hunting white tailed deer during fifteen years residence in Wisconsin.

DEDICATION

First and foremost I dedicate this book to our Creator Jesus Christ. I am grateful to Him for the great outdoors and all it includes; the hummingbirds, elk, streams, forests, mountains, the universe and all He has done for me on the cross and in my life

Next it is dedicated to my Dad Elby French who first introduced me to the outdoors, to my wife Suzie for graciously putting up with my absences. It is dedicated to my family, to my son Steve, a "natural born killer" and a superior hunter. It is dedicated also to my grandchildren, some of whom are "natural born killers," as well.

As I write this I am sitting at a pool just below my home. The pool is supplied with water from rain and snow melt off the roof. This is dry country and right now there are Robins, Clark's Nutcrackers, Solitaires, Juncos, all kinds of song birds drinking and bathing in it. Maybe fifty birds or more. Deer come evenings. bobcats, lions, lynx, bears, coyotes and maybe an occasional elk come to drink. Hallelujah!

HUNTING AND SCOUTING SKILLS

HOW DID YOU DO THAT?

At the request of a mutual friend I took a guy who was an outdoor writer with limited hunting experience on a scouting trip up in central Wisconsin in February of 1973. Before hand I went over a topographical map with him saying, "There will be a deer trail here, there and here, etc." He and I didn't know each other well yet and I had never been to this spot before. We hiked in through a snow of about six inches deep on a sunny day. As we went to the spots where I told him there would be deer trails and found them exactly where I said they would be within ten feet of where I said from the topographic map. Finally he said apparently somewhat amazed, "How did you do that?" I was somewhat full of myself from his statement. However, actually I had every confidence about what I demonstrated. I call it, "Transferal of knowledge." Or "translating patterns." Once you learn a pattern of something you can transfer that knowledge to other similar areas or situations. I had learned from other hunts in central Wisconsin that Whitetail Deer make trails that run around the perimeter of low places like marshes, ponds, bogs, etc. These trails are about ten to twenty feet out on dry ground and go all the way around any such terrain. They also make trails that go directly across a marsh most often at the narrowest spots. They also make trails on ridges, (such as they are in that country) as well as trails where cover comes to points like two arrowheads of brush pointing at each other, etc.

Noting my friend's amazement, and being a ham, I decided to capitalize on his wonder. I had a small stainless pot the sides of which I had flattened so it would fit in a plastic lunch box were I kept food and other gear and also used as a seat. He was taking copious notes for his newspaper. He looked inquiringly at the pot which looks a bit like a small WWII German helmet. I was a member of a missionary group which worked in South America as well as all over the world. I said, "You know the Nazis were in South America during WWII. Some headhunters killed some of them and shrunk this guy's head with his helmet on." He pushed me off my seat into the snow and we have been fast friends ever since. He listens with jaundiced ears ever since then.

8

Notes

GRIZZLY BEAR FINDS MY TROPHY

My forty-five pound Keeshond dog " Grizzly Bear" and I took three days to scout for elk here in Colorado in June of 2004. We had hiked up to about 11,000 feet altitude. It was steep and we rested often. We had just sit down under some pines. The under story was sparse and I could see about fifty to one hundred yards under the trees. Griz growled and I quietly shushed her. I looked to our right and here came two bull elk. The lead bull was a trophy. They were in the velvet and their antlers were only about one third grown. I managed to grab the camera and got off a few seconds of video of the second bull which was considerably smaller, but a five point.

We watched them sidle on down the mountain's dry gulch. I thought, "strange that they would be going 'down' at 9 am." We went on up the mountain and spent two nights camped up top by a pond near timberline. I squirreled away the encounter with the two bulls along with notes for my maps and GPS coordinates, of trails, springs, sign, etc. for future reference. I had been told that some of the largest bulls in Colorado lived in this unit. Also there were always hundreds of elk on their winter feeding grounds on both sides of a nearby state highway and over the range to the west.

I began to do more research in Colorado's Department of Wildlife regulations and applying for a license as the area is a draw unit. In 2006 I received the license desired.

Having lots of ambition and energy, I hunted two other areas up north near Steamboat Springs getting good opportunities at two legal bulls however I only had a cow license for bow. I then drove to the unit I had a draw for and climbed until I busted a small five point bull about 5 pm, September 4th. I sat down and listened. I could hear an occasional bugle above, in the direction where I had encountered the two bulls in June of 2004. I was thinking that the elk may have been going down in mid mornings to find the head of a spring. I had hiked up the mountain deliberately loaded light; no tent, sleeping bag, etc. After dark I bedded down on some pine cone shucks where squirrels had made a mass of made a mass of these under a fir tree. The night was cool and dry, but not miserable. It was probably about forty degrees. I could hear elk bugling to my south all night as they worked their way down to feed for the night.

It was September the 5th the next morning. I mention the date because they obviously were beginning to rut. This year (2008) they were not bugling even by September 10th, perhaps due to bears. The 5th was warm and scouting to the south and up I found a sub-ridge which didn't show much promise. The main ridge is quite wide and runs up to a point at about 11,500 feet. Back down it broadens at the base of the mountain to a spread of maybe a mile wide. The slope of this set of peaks ranges to the southeast in general. It is about 10,000 feet in altitude at it's base. The slope is "cut" by many sub ridges. As I climbed the ridge it became barren under mid sized Aspens with sparse undercover and difficult footing as it became very steep. Tiring, I sat down and pondered what to do. I noticed many interlacing elk trails however in this area.

By this time I'd been hunting about 10 days total and had responsibilities at home weighing the mind. It becomes difficult to keep up a positive attitude and a certain "tiredness" can set in. More on this later.

Carefully working back down the north side of the ridge it softened into more gentle terrain but then steepened into a 45 degree slope with thick "dog hair" spruce. Continuing back towards the stream there was an arrow stuck in a small tree, giving evidence of another hunter giving it try a couple years before. Soon I found a small steep meadow. The most notable feature in the meadow is that underground water is in it. A spring emerges directly out of the side of the ridge heading a creek. I've never seen anything quite like it. This, I believe is the water the preceding bulls were going down to in 2004.

Feeling I set up with my small seat in the midst of the meadow and elderberries and spent the day watching, listening, etc. When the winds shifted downhill about 4:00pm I relocated to the bottom of the beautiful meadow. Elk trails wind through it from several directions. The spring makes a sweet melody. Elderberries occupy the top half. Aspens and spruce adorn the surrounding forest. It is a paradise. I set up with total

11

camouflage, scent hiding clothing, a sheet type blind and settled in for the evening's ambush. About an hour later a mature cow elk appeared to my right. Because I had been careless with scent earlier in the day she smelled me and balked. She was thirsty however and hung around for a long time, barking occasionally until the coming events unfolded. Around 6 pm I heard rocks rolling in the direction from which I had entered the meadow about 10 am. The rock sounds were accompanied by a deep moaning loud GROWL! Knowing what this meant I stood up. Surrounded by thick trees on 3 sides I was nearly invisible. A nice 5x6 bull was running with two cows and calves. The herd went directly to the spring but I could barely make them out due to the cover. They drank and fed on the lush herbage. Immediately four smaller bulls showed themselves up in the elderberries where I had spent the day. All were shooters but not near the size of the growling bull. They were totally oblivious to my scent being engrossed in each other and their rutting rituals. The 5x6 didn't like all the competition and charged up a steep loose dirt trail to run the other bulls off. Elk were all over the place. On this hunt I was aiming to take any legal elk, even the cow to the right, until the large bull showed up. I was glad she didn't present a good shot now.

The bull went behind a tall blue spruce. As he did I drew the bow. He emerged to its' right at 43 yards at an up hill angle of near 40 degrees. He stopped and looked me "in the eye". I put the 35 yard pin on his heart. When he looked back to his front at the other bulls I touched the release trigger. The string slapped my arm. (I had been trimming the leafy camo jacket arm for days trying to solve that). The arrow flew "straight as an arrow" but the bull jumped the string due to the arm guard slap. The arrow struck him through the hind quarters and he charged on up the trail into aspens and spruce. I could see a large dark spot in the middle of his hind quarters as he took off. The rest of the herd milled about some but hung close by. A small 5 point stood off to my right at just 20 yards seeming to be almost unaware of my presence. The first cow continued to bark off to the right and moved further back and up into the aspens. In a few minutes the other cows and calves moved on down stream apparently never aware of me, the remaining bulls following. After a few minutes I climbed uphill to where the 5x6 was last seen. In the trail laid half the arrow and beyond was a large splash of blood maybe 12 inches in diameter. I trailed the blood maybe 15 yards but being "gunshy" due to previous good hits and seeing elk get away I decided to wait until morning to follow up. Night was falling and I retreated back under the spruce to sleep. After a cool night I continued the track about 6:30am and found the bull about 150 yards beyond. The arrow had pierced both hams and clipped the gut just enough to allow any gases to escape. The night was cool and in fact it snowed a bit as I dressed out the kill. After boning out the meat it took about 3 days and 6 round trips to backpack it all to the camper. Total miles; about 21 miles: largely off trail. "Always shoot them uphill", as my Uncle told me. Some of that bull is still in the freezer. It is the best elk meat I've ever eaten. I spent some of my hunt this year in the same spot. There was virtually no sign and no bugling. The elk were apparently all over the mountain or somewhere else. That's elk hunting.

Another hunter I met later e-mailed me that ranchers had come in the last weekend of bow season and ridden all over gathering up cattle. The elk were bugling all over but disappeared during the roundup. You would wish for more consideration. On further thought I'm wondering wether bears were responsible for the elk being other places earlier. The other hunter saw a huge black bear. I saw a "tri-colored" black bear during the early days of September. Also someone told me that cattlemen pushing cows had seen an 8x9 point bull in the same area after season. There is a sign on the main highway within a few miles nearby saying, "CAUTION ELK CROSSING".

COMPUTER HUNTING

I'm quite certain this is common practice these days but here's my angle on it. For the last several years I've learned to begin my search for a good elk hunting area on the computer. The Shearer Corporation publishes a great Atlas of Colorado and several other states with excellent topographic maps. They are good enough to replace or augment the USGS topographical maps, available now on computer disks. The beauty of the "Roads of Colorado" by Shearer is that it shows in color code what property is public and private with about ten different designations. You can easily determine where the public lands are and of what kind they are; wilderness, National Forest, private, Bureau of Land Management, etc. Also I use the topographic maps now available on CDs . However I generally begin a search in the Colorado Department of Parks and Wildlife's Big Game regulations. Taking the Colorado DP&W regulation maps and comparing it along with some map of the state I have picked out new locations. They use "GMUs", Game Management Units. I pick a GMU based on the species, method of take, general location and times of hunt. Example; Unit 2 in Moffat County, archery, either sex, August 30- September 28th, 2008. This is a "draw" hunt so I need to get my application to the DP&W by April 1st for example. This can be done on-line or by mail. At first flush the regs. are confusing, however, again, to simplify your search first identify the species you wish to hunt, then the general area and method of hunting and ignore the rest of the information. However read and know the laws. After some thought it isn't all that complex. If you live out of state and have never hunted elk it can seem daunting at first. If you live out of state and hunt here from time to time know that the rules can change some each year. Colorado is currently the only state in the union that offers over the counter elk licenses. If you are going for a draw unit be sure to get the regs early. The draw closes April 1st currently. Plan early.

Having picked an area you wish to hunt it is best to make at least one scouting trip before season. If you live close enough this isn't too difficult and enjoyable as a summer fishing or hiking trip. If it is not possible to pre-scout an area plan to "waste" a season going into an area "green" or go in several days ahead to look, quietly.

CAUTION AGAIN: one of the biggest reasons elk leave an area is people roaming around in their haunts. Pre scout in this manner with care or they will leave. A terrific source of information is Google Earth or Virtual Earth. The power of these Internet tools is awesome. I like to print out a couple of satellite views of a new area. It gives you a great look at a prospective spot. It's usually not as good as aerials but is inexpensive and again, Terrific! Having done your "paperwork" and landed on a prospective area and then going to that area and finding elk is great adventure. Late June or July would be the best times to scout. I advise picking about three areas to scout so that if one doesn't pan out you can go to another. I use a computer map program and pick out a likely spot, transfer the coordinates into my GPS then plan a hike into that area to see on the ground what the prospects are. I located a spring on "Mystery Mountain" a few years ago on a CD topographical map and put the coordinates in my GPS. The nifty little device took me to within ten feet of it. Again no specific spots are published in this book because if I did and a hundred people showed up at that spot you might want my neck in a noose. Right? Recently a young clerk in a store in Colorado Springs told me about his family sitting on a highway for forty-five minutes waiting for a herd of elk to cross. He said there were hundreds of them. I have cataloged that tip in my mind and have followed the above process to, at least, give it a look.

LIST OF "PAPER HUNTING-COMPUTER HUNTING" OPTIONS

* Elk concentrations map in this book
* This book
* Full color prints from the Colorado DP&W's NDIS maps
* The Roads of Colorado Atlas, Shearer Publishing
* Appropriate Topographic maps
* Colorado Dept. Of Parks and Wildlife regulations
* Google Earth glossy prints. (Glossy prints will show details best)

HUMMINGBIRD BULLS

In the early 1970s I had been trailing two five point bulls through a mix of aspen, Engelmann firs, ridges and meadows. We had been playing "hide and seek" for about forty-five minutes. The bulls weren't aware of my presence. I was using a 45pound Bear Kodiak recurve bow I had owned since about 1958. I had shot a coyote with it in 1960 at three yards and hunted whitetail deer in Wisconsin with it. I had a bow quiver with five arrows. It is a far cry from my single cam bows. I still own that old Kodiak. My first whitetail buck fell to it's power one foggy Wisconsin morning. The fletching was bright orange natural feathers. I fletched my own at that time.

The bulls fed and meandered through the dark timber down to a beaver pond, water, and grass. Then they wandered back into the dark timber.

The two bulls eventually moseyed out into the green aspens and sunlight about 8:45 am. I was behind and to their right, hidden at the edge of the dark timber. They emerged from the dark timber at about forty-five yards. I raised my bow and began to draw. Just then a male Broadtailed Hummingbird buzzed the orange feathers on the arrows in the bow quiver. He then landed on the arrow I was about to draw, right in front of the bow. I thought, "Pal, you are about to go for the ride of your life." Of course, as I drew, he took off. The bulls were going away at forty-five yards. They were both "shooters". I settled my bow sight's forty-five yard pin on the last bull and let go.

I had long struggled with, gold shy, which is a mental glitch for some archers where they can not settle the sight on the bull's eye. For me, it has always been hanging up a bit to the left. The new compound bows help that immensely.   The bull was slowly walking to my right and with "Gold Shy" unconquered the arrow struck the bull in the hip bone. Two inches to the right and the arrow would have gone through the bull's flank right into the heart and lung area. The arrow only stuck hard in the hip bone and off they ran, no mortal wound. If you've never wounded one and lost it you have not been hunting long or have been privileged to hunt in ideal conditions.

The hummingbird made that hunt special. I have done an oil painting titled: CHECK IT OUT based on that experience. You can see it at www.edfrench.fineaw.com

Focus: In my experience of often traveling in from out of state, there was a necessary mental shift that sometimes is hard to make quickly. Know this: that you may only get one opportunity at a good shot in a week's hunt. Being mentally sharp and focused is very important. Take field points and practice during the middle of the day with a few shots into a good soft background. Be ready. If you get more than one good opportunity on a public land hunt during a week's hunt, consider yourself very fortunate. The success rate with a bow is lower than with a rifle but the adventure factor is far higher.

Note; spruce, fir and pines, etc. are known in the west as "dark timber" because it is dark, full of shade, even so thick in "downed timber" that at times you can't see beyond the end your arm. Once up on "Hum-de-hum Ridge" hunting with Pop, a cow elk stepped past me at close range. I could have slapped her on the rump. She was legal. We were rifle hunting. I followed her ASAP but did not see her again due to the extremely thick "dog hair" spruce. Within two steps she just disappeared. "light timber" is also known as quakies or aspen. Quakies because the leaves quake at even the lightest breeze. "light timber" because it is open underneath and full of sunlight. Aspen bark is a light vanilla color. In mid to late September that light is awesome. The leaves have at least fifteen different colors of yellow, green, orange, red, brown, blue, purple, etc. in the Fall. When the leaves are falling and carpet the forest floor it is like walking in a cathedral of paradise. I love it.

ELK SIGNS

ELK SIGN AND SOUNDS

Elk leave signs of their presence and like a detective you can observe these and make sense of it and increase your chances of success. They are often quiet as cats but do leave tracks, trails and make sounds that can tip you off to their whereabouts.The highway departments sometimes have signs up on the highway, warning of the presence of elk. These mean something: **elk are in the area.**

CHEW: Elk chew the bark of aspen trunks. Apparently this is done largely in the winter but can occur at any time. In places the normally vanilla white aspen bark is blackened with these scars. This can be seen from a long distance and is a clue as to the presence of elk in the area. Fresher chews are green to brown. Sometimes the blackened tree trunks are starkly dramatic, but if you aren't looking carefully, they can be missed.

TRAILS: elk trails are about one foot wide but generally are not pounded down to clear dirt as much or quite as wide as cattle trails. A herd of domestic cattle can clear a trail in one pass that a blind man can follow. Elk are sometimes seen in the company of cattle and do not seem to be overly bothered by their presence. If cattle have been allowed to over graze an area I have found elk sign sparse in such conditions. I personally don't like to see cattle or sheep on a hunting trip but they are a fact of life. I stopped at one camp of hunters hunkering in camp during a wet September snow storm near a nice camp fire. They told me that Basque sheep herders came to their camp urging, "Come shoot the elk, they are running in among our sheep and striking at them with their feet, come shoot the elk." Elk make various kinds of trails: cruising trails, bedding trails, feeding trails, migration trails, etc. I look for trails that lead from feed to bedding areas. Trails generally run diagonally up and down the sides of ridges, through saddles and at times along ridge tops or just under ridge tops in timber or otherwise. Trails may not be very obvious if the foliage is thick because the particular climate you are in is wet.

RUBS; bulls rub young pines and firs about two to six inches in diameter. They also "attack" willows, sometimes in their testosterone driven rages. I once stood along a road side in Yellowstone National Park and watched a large six point bull strip all the bark off a four inch thick Lodgepole pine, bend it over and essentially kill it in about two minutes. Rubs are done about August when the velvet dries, splits and falls off the matured antlers. Deer generally rub about a month later.

TRACKS: the tracks of elk are about two to three times as large as deer and rounder. They can be confused with those of cattle calves at times. The mass of an elk track is about three times that of a deer in square inches. Tracks are seen on trails, of course, and wherever they go. Depending on the conditions they are in and time passed since laid down they are either obvious or very hard to see. Walking into the low sun early or late in the day helps you see tracks better. If it's dark holding a flashlight low to the ground to cast a side light helps.

This is the "SECRET" hidden in this book and in the elk forests.

STEAMIN' GREEN, THE REAL SCOOP ON ELK POOP.

DROPPINGS: Elk defecate pill shaped droppings which are larger than deer but similar in shape. Their droppings are about one half the size of moose. These are a dead give away as to their past presence. My high school hunting buddy and I used to tell each other, "If you'll eat a handful of those you will be a lot smarter, they are called 'Smart Pills'." And I reckon you would be. What can I say? We were high school boys. Seriously, a smart elk hunter is a student of elk droppings. Here lies the hidden secret of finding that big bull. This is the "secret" hidden within the pages of this book but more importantly in the elk mountains. If all the other signs fail you this one will not. A friend from New York state I met on a hunt about 1998 in Colorado and I titled it, "Steamin' Green". After wasting a season or two in good elk country but not finding this vital sign I developed the **POLICY** of keep going until you see "Steamin' Green." In Colorado elk, during good summers eat lots of succulent herbage. The result is that they drop piles of "elk pies" something like cow pies, but smaller. Elk droppings during bow season run from "wads" of tight pellets about a fist size to these "pies" that can be as large as eight inches in diameter. They are finer in composition than cattle droppings and the fresher they are the greener and shinier they look. Domestic sheep leave an elongated shape, again: deer droppings are similar to elk but smaller. This past Fall bow hunt I saw moose droppings. They are about twice the size of elk, about 1 ½ inches long and I've never seen them in many colors but a milky orange is normal as moose feed mostly on willow. I know I'm writing "dirty" here but it is a prime secret to finding elk, especially getting "bow close".

Later in October when the frosts have killed the herbage and the moisture content of elk feed is greatly diminished, elk droppings are drier and pelletized to about ¾ to one inch in length. Droppings are effected by weather and time. What you are looking for is a soft green dropping that shines and smells. "This morning's droppings." If you aren't seeing these, keep going as the elk are most likely not there at this time. When you see this vital sign, slow down, focus, get ready, hunt carefully! September, 1995, on opening day I parked the Trooper several miles in on a very "ifi" four wheel road, several miles in from a gravel county road. Taking my backpack, I intended to hunt between two major creeks in a basically east facing area below a complex of high mountain peaks. There is a major National Forest trail from south to north there. Avoiding this trail I packed around it to the east and up through steep parks, willows and firs. As I topped out over the rim of a bowl through which the horse trail meandered below, I spotted a spike and cows below. It was mid afternoon. I backed off and changed into hunting clothes, then continued to try and put the sneak on them. After a few minutes of this a cow spotted me from about seventy- five yards. She barked loudly and elk ran everywhere. I estimate there were about sixty of them. A very nice 6x6 bull was in charge, it seemed. The whole herd thundered up the mountain to the west. I began to explore the area and try to learn what I could. On a forested hill above the main park and trail, the elk sign and smell was so thick it was almost nauseating.

There was an elk pie about every five square yards. Elk beds were thick as fleas. The herd had obviously spent several days in the area. No one had walked or ridden the trail below to disturb them. This is an unusual example of elk sign. I prefer to get up on only a few elk because there are fewer eyes and ears to detect you.

BEDS: Elk like deer, make beds. These range in permanence from just one time use to, apparently, centuries of use. The permanent ones are often in shaded cool north slopes on small flat spots. I'm thinking of one which almost always has sign in it. It looks like they have bedded there forever. If an animal has been there recently there will be impressions of its' hooves, legs, body and usually urine. It will smell like elk. A bed is about five feet long and three feet wide. They will sometimes circle round and round, pawing the sticks and rocks out of the spot to make it more comfortable. The forest duff will be churned to a finer mulch than the surrounding floor. Sometimes these beds are right in the middle of a trail. They are as flat as the terrain will allow. The beds are generally in the same areas year after year. Often 5-10 yards below a ridge on a south facing slope in shade away from disturbing daily winds.

SMELL: The odor of elk is unlike that of cattle in that it is pleasant, at least to an elk hunter. Once you know it you look forward to finding it and it is a good clue that elk are close or have been recently. The smell is similar to the "faded" odor of a Sanford brand dry marker or can be likened to cattle but not as strong. It smells like cattle a bit, with an apple mash taint. Hard to describe.Once you smell it you won't forget.

WALLOWS; Bulls roll and splash in muddy wallows, cooling their overheated bodies and impressing other bulls and cows with this display and the resulting appearance. Active wallows differ greatly in location, size and water content. They range from ponds to just bathtub sized sinks. One thing they all have in common is, of course, water. They may be out in a park or hidden in a small niche in the woods where there is a seep. Setting up an ambush in the afternoon heat may pay out with a good opportunity for an exciting shot, crosswind of one of these.

SOUNDS: One of the pleasant aspects of hunting is sound. As you no doubt know it's quiet, but it's not really. These sounds are good for the soul. Witness the "sigh" of the wind in the pines, the soft "rattle" of aspens leaves, "quakies." In the forest Clark's nutcrackers come to a pool just below my home/studio to drink and bathe. Their grated cat like calls are one of the most pleasant songs in the high mountains. I love it. It's one of the reasons we head away from civilization and into God's great outdoors. Other birds make many sounds. Flickers make a call which is easy to mistake for a cow elk call until you've heard it some. Elk are usually cat like quiet, however when they do make sounds it is electrifying. They **mew** like large cats, **snap limbs, thump their hooves** on dead fall, grind their teeth, making a **chirping** sound like small birds. The bulls and on rare occasions, the cows **bugle**. The bulls **growl, bellow** like a Hereford bull, **whistle,** and again, of course **bugle** in that magic way hunters and nature lovers admire. Elk **cough**. 2004 rifle season I had an extra tag for a cow. I had set up under a low fir on a ridge over a large park. A stream and elk trails were below. It was opening morning. About 7:45 am I heard a **loud cough** to my right. This was a location which was not convenient to watch. Looking in that direction I spotted seventeen elk feeding my direction. I probably shot too quick, being concerned that other hunters might be close, but scratch one cow. At the shot two hunters appeared from my left! Elk **bark** like a giant dog when alarmed. It usually means they aren't sure of something they have seen. I've never heard them **bark** if they've smelled me. If they smell you they are GONE! Listen for the sounds. They tell you something. On opening day about 1970 I had made my way from camp to the top of a large sagebrush covered park. This season cows were not legal until the third day. I had been in the aspens along a jeep trail for about four hundred yards. It was 8:30 in the morning. I heard a **loud cat- like mewing**. It went on and on. I thought it might be a cougar. I crept over a small grassy ridge and below me about fifty yards a nice fat cow elk was moseying along making these calls. I backed up next to a small group of three large aspens. She wound her way right past me. I was fully camouflaged. She was totally unaware of my presence at about two feet and I was tempted to slap her on the rump but didn't want to disturb the situation or get kicked. These are the experiences that make bow hunting elk the wonder it is. Nineteen-ninety-five it snowed about the fifth day of bow season. I had climbed about a mile from the road along familiar trails in the aspens and firs to a spot where I had in a previous year shot a bull with a muzzle loader. I sat for a while, listening and waiting for sunrise. The moon shown on the snow. It was an eire but tantalizing atmosphere. A call drifted through the forest. "What is that," I thought. It went on and on for about twenty minutes. It didn't sound quite like an elk but sort of like an elk and a pig or bird mixed together. I wondered about that for several years then my wife and I had the opportunity to spend several weeks in our RV parked near a small mountain zoo. One morning I awoke to the same sound. Investigating I found a cougar repeatedly calling in the same way. The zoo keeper told me it was the mating call of cougars. The summer of 1958 I was a lumberjack above Eagle, Colorado. One weekend I hiked above camp into a large burn and towards the high peaks to the east. On the way back on Sunday afternoon I was tired and walking carelessly through the woods back to camp. I idly and carelessly jumped up on a large dead tree laying in a meadow mixed with timber. I kicked large limbs off the tree as I walked down its' length. Suddenly I heard a loud limb snap to my left. As I stepped off the top of the tree I looked into the face of a five point bull. Other elk were present. Because my racket sounded just like theirs, they weren't alarmed at all! As he saw me, off they ran. When hunting elk you can often get away with snapping small limbs and making other racket. Elk and deer are panicked by motion they see with silence as that is what a lion sounds like: silence. Another elk sound; **pounding hooves and crashing of large bodies and antlers through timber.** This sound helped me get my bull elk opening day of rifle season 1959. I had set up on a rocky point overlooking a large area of parks, rock slides and mixed timber. About 7 am; **crash bang** here they came. A herd had been spooked by another hunter and was heading towards me on a well used trail I had scouted the day before just under the cliffs. BANG; tag filled. The sounds they made as they ran allowed me to set up in time to make the shots. Things can happen fast on an elk hunt and they certainly did that day.

SUMMARY OF SOME ELK SIGNS

* ROAD SIGNS
* ASPEN TREE TRUNK CHEWS
* STEAMIN' GREEN AND OTHER DROPS
* TRAILS
* RUBS
* BEDS
* WALLOWS
* SOUNDS
*SMELLS

ONE OF MY FAVORITE ELK STAND SET UPS

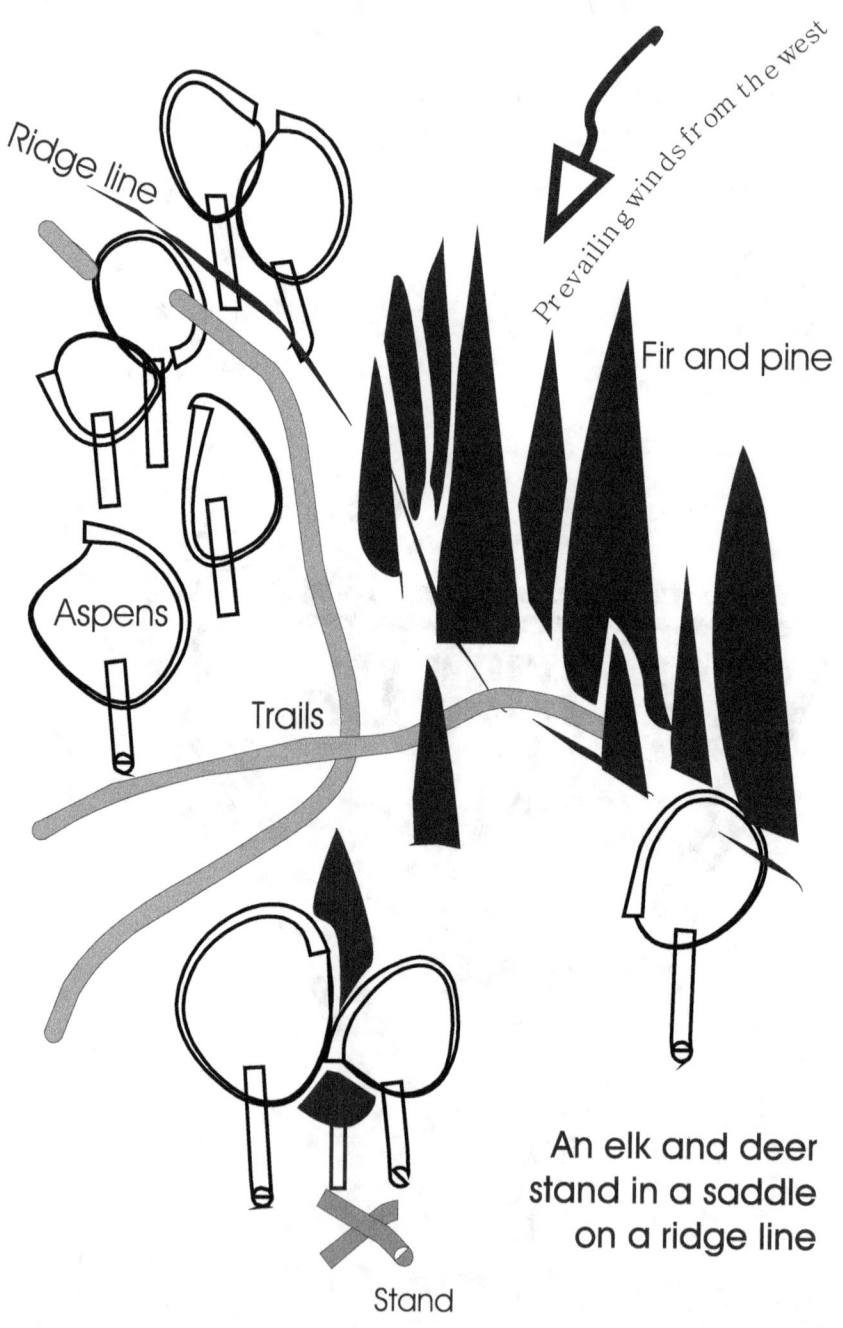

Ridge line

Prevailing winds from the west

Fir and pine

Aspens

Trails

An elk and deer
stand in a saddle
on a ridge line

Stand

A QUICK START GUIDE TO JUDGING BULL ELK

Learn to judge the size of elk in the field by thinking through, ahead of time, at a zoo or in a protected area like a national park.

Top photo; Notice that if you could draw a line down from the back of his antlers that it would come just behind his withers. This is a six point, very respectable bull.

This is also a six point bull but the mass of his antlers isn't as thick. If he were to tip his head up the back of his antlers would come back to about the "center" of his shoulder blades. This is a shooter but not near the bull the top one is. Notice that his belly line is flat, not bulged down as the top bull. This probably indicates that he has been breeding and has lost some weight.

The difference in these two bulls is obvious from this frontal viewpoint. The top bull is a five point. The bottom one is a six point but a much smaller elk. .

Top; Antlers from a bull Dad shot in 1955. They measure 342 with heavy mass. Dad shot the bull in the heart with one 150 grain bullet as it ran at about 100 yards across a large park with the "Meat Wagon", a sporterized 30-06 Enfield. The bull was following a cow and calf at high noon! This was on public land in northern Colorado.

Right; One of the author's antler collections. The largest is his 2006 bull shot with a bow in a draw unit. Also shown on back cover.

31

WHAT IS A TROPHY BULL?

You may be meat hunting, trophy hunting or with an attitude of a combination of these in mind. Personally that has varied for me from year to year.

Note: Some of the best elk meat I've ever had is from the bull whose antlers are shown on page 31 . A caution to those who illegally kill a bull, take only the antlers and then also shoot a cow, thinking the bull is not good eating. Ethical hunters will turn you in. The Colorado Division of Parks and Wildlife will take your money, your guns and your hunting privileges from you. The Division published, a while back, the story of a sting on several hunters in the Wimineuche Wilderness who were fined, in total, about $65,000. They lost their guns and some lost hunting privileges, nationwide, as I recall, for life. One guy was sentenced to prison time. Hunt ethically.

Back to what is a trophy. You have probably heard the adage, that "a trophy is what it is to you." After hunting elk for many years I spent a week in 1994 studying elk at Horseshoe Park in Rocky Mountain National Park above Estes Park, Colorado. Bulls would bugle in response to a squeaky windshield wiper. After watching them there and in the rest of the park under non-hunting conditions for a week I developed a better appreciation of what a large bull elk really is. As a young hunter back in the 1950s, the attitude was, If it's an elk, shoot it. Going up from the Denver area to the mountains on rare opportunities and just seeing them kind of dazzled my mind. Also due to overcrowded hunting at that time and different regulations you shot one as soon as you could and went over to see what you got. Watching elk, undisturbed in a park situation like Yellowstone for several days helps you develop an understanding of what you are seeing in the forests. Seeing them in a zoo and giving this all some thought helps you to evaluate them in the woods.

Thanks to the larger herds and spread out seasons, elk in Colorado don't seem to be under the intense opening day pressure they were decades ago and I personally have been able to pass some up. It's a good feeling. Also being an artist, painting elk helps me to study them and know what I'm seeing. It takes an attitude adjustment. The more you see elk the better you will know them. You will learn the difference between a mature healthy cow and a lumpy old hag in her last years. Yep, saw one: grey, lumpy, old.

There are five point bulls and there are five point bulls. Six point bulls are not all alike. If you see two six points in Moraine Park in Rocky Mountain National Park for example in late September and can compare them you may see that although the amount of tines are the same, one bull could be the other's granddad. To appreciate this under hunting conditions is valuable knowledge if you are trophy hunting. Even on public lands in the National Forests of Colorado **there are still trophy bulls out there.**

In fifty or so years of elk hunting, always on public land I have encountered about five actual "trophy bulls" and brought one home with the bow. I have a set of antlers from a bull Dad shot in 1955 which he shot with the "Meat Wagon", a running shot at about one hundred fifty yards. One shot in the heart near timberline on public land. It is a 6x6. It scores 342.5 inches. The bull I shot with the bow in 2006 scores 242.75 inches. It is a 5x6 with additional little Rocky Mountain points. Rocky mountain points are in the same position as the brow tines on a deer and above an elk's brow tines. Some cowboys jumped an 8x9 in the same area where I hunted this past September, 2008.

Again: there are still huge bulls out there on public land. I hope you bring one home some day. Again this book is intended for first time or inexperienced elk hunters in Colorado and other elk states. If you really want a big trophy bull "now" and have lots of cash then a guided ranch hunt is the ticket. I've watched some television hunts where you know the hunter spent from five thousand to twenty thousand dollars or so and bagged a monster. I saw one hunt on tv where the guide and hunter fiddled with a gun tripod, binoculars, talked him over, etc. for about a minute. The bull stood there and stared at them from maybe eighty yards then they finally got set they shot this Hereford, whoops, elk. Shot on a private ranch hunt. I was privilege to hunt nilgai (a large antelope from India imported to south Texas in the early 1900s) on the Kenedy Ranch. Great fun. I would love to be able to spend the thousands it takes to hunt a trophy bull in Canada on a guided hunt. Most of us cannot afford the large sums it costs to hunt the private hunts and so this book.

Knowing what to expect ahead of time will give you an advantage. What you are going to see in Colorado's public forests nine times out of ten is spikes, rag horns, and mid sized five point bulls. An uncle I used to hunt with had a couple sayings which I found frustrating but true; "there is a lot of room around an elk," and, "elk are where you find them." Another saying of his I've found very useful: "always shoot them up hill." It's easier to carry them out.

Getting used to elk in a national park setting or zoo helps with elk fever. I was privileged to hunt with a friend in southern Colorado in 1993 who is an expert hunter and guide. He taught me more in two afternoons about "elk psychology" than I had learned on my own and by reading magazines in thirty years. He called in a real nice five point which bolted at forty yards. I was shaking so much that the arrow fell off the rest twice. Somehow with age and experience I seem cured of "elk fever." You can't hit them if the arrow falls off the rest! A note again on how to see a bull. A bull which has been rutting intensely may lose up to 30% of his body weight. A bull in this condition has a flat look to his belly from the bottom of the rib cage back. He looks lean and he is. A bull which is just coming into rut has a full, fat, healthy look. The rut is intense and some bulls don't survive it. Some die of exhaustion and starvation during the winter. Save a bull from such a sad fate. Shoot him.

One year I had decided to hunt for a BIG bull only. I had flown in from Florida late at night, rented a car at Stapleton Airport in Denver and had driven up to ten thousand feet altitude and hiked up near eleven thousand feet. The next morning it was cool for September. It was close to frosty. Not having the calling experience I wanted but giving it another try I crept to a good vantage point and knelt down in the aspens. I had a video camera on my chest. I called briefly. I heard a really lousy sounding response about one hundred-fifty yards up to the west. I looked that direction and saw what appeared to be the limb of a compound bow coming my way. I thought, "oh no, some other hunter is in here." Soon a nice five point bull made his way to within fifteen yards of me. The bow limbs were actually his antlers. He stopped and surveyed in my direction. He was looking for the "bull" which had just called to him. He was only an average bull so I videoed him and let him go. What a trophy is, is up to you. Other years I would have been glad to shoot him. I didn't get an elk that year but still enjoyed the trip.

Notes

CALLING ALL ELK

Before a guide friend taught me how to call elk I would go out and try to sound like the biggest bull in the woods. It never worked. We went just a few miles from his home near Pagosa Springs. He would call like a small bull, we waited for a response and then walked towards the answer and stalked to about three hundred yards away, watched the winds and continued to call using cow calls and the small bull sounds. It worked, not every time, but it worked. He would call less and like a smaller bull as we moved in. Then we would set up, with myself secreted as much as possible, he would retreat maybe fifty yards and hope the challenger would come in.

This is common knowledge now but not so back in the 1950s. I went out the next morning alone and called and a large calf almost ran over me. Spikes and younger bulls will come in quite readily. A lot has been learned by hunters about calling since the 1950s. Some guys used to call using a whistle sometimes made out of plastic pipe. Calling has become much more sophisticated in the past twenty years and it's hard to tell another hunter from an elk at times. Calls are superior to the past as well as all other equipment, bows, etc.

Back about 1973 on "Mystic Ridge" in the Gore Range in Colorado I could hear a bull bugling maybe ¼ mile to the south. I bugled back repeatedly but he would not move. It was about 2 pm and very warm. I stalked closer and discovered a herd bedded down for the day under some fir trees. The bull would bugle back but because he was "asleep" for the day he would not get up and leave the herd to come to a call. Unfortunately there was about a fifty yard open space between us and when I approached they saw me and off they went.

This was in one of the summer concentrations shown on the maps. It is historically full of elk but unfortunately the word is out and by the second morning of bow season they are so spooked by hunters acting foolishly that it is not very productive. What I'm illustrating is that the chances of them coming to a call is that, a chance but it's great sport. Get a good call, practice, listen to recordings and have a great time. Watching the outdoor television programs can put you way ahead of where I was at that time, in mind set. Elk hunting is a mind game.

ELK PSYCHOLOGY

As testosterone levels rise, peak and wane, different bulls come into rut, full rut and go out. A bull in peak rut may readily come to a call, "full bore", alert, looking for action, but that is the best it gets. Another bull which has not come into rut or exhausted himself and gone out may not be interested at all. Another may sneak in downwind, catch your scent and you may never see him. Different bulls come into rut at different times. It doesn't all happen at once. They are active day and night at times like this.

I once slept within two to three hundred yards of a bull that sounded big. He kept me awake all night bugling but would not come in to a call the next day. I never saw him and I'm guessing he had cows with him.

NOTE; Rut is an old French word which means "roaring". If you've hunted red deer or heard them on a television program you know they do roar, whereas elk bugle. The word rut sticks however and describes the breeding season for many of the deer family. The rut for elk generally starts as early as late August until early October depending on many factors. In Colorado it is generally understood that it peaks starting about the first full moon of September which roughly corresponds with when the aspens are turned fully yellow and the first frosts of Autumn. It seems to really get going about the third week of September. However nothing is a sure deal. Theses are only guidelines.

To call an elk into bow range is one of the most exhilarating experiences an elk hunter can have. That bull wants cows. He doesn't want to duke it out with another bull. If he thinks he can take them away from some amateur and his testosterone is up, he very well may come in looking to run the "kid" off. The psychology involved is to try and think like he does. Try to imagine what he is doing, what he wants. Generally call like a small bull, a lot of cows, a spike or two.

I've read that pouring water from a canteen on a rock and making a splashing sound will sometimes trigger them to come if they hang up. Scraping a tree with a branch and perhaps pounding the ground with the branch may work as well. Try to sound like a herd of cows needing a "big daddy" to take care of business. One hunter accidentally called in a bull just breaking branches for firewood.

Great Pyrenees dogs sleeping in my "camp" 2001

ELK HUNTING DOGS

For several years I had hunted an area in which sheep herders kept their flocks. Occasionally they would bring them through "my" area. I encountered them with mixed emotions.

One afternoon I was setting against an Engelmann spruce around 6pm hoping to see something. I was watching a large park with steep slopes to the west and streams running through it. From my right dashed a coyote about fifteen yards out as though the devil his own self was on his tail. I wondered, of course, what's the matter? I peaked out of my hiding spot. Up to the right about five hundred yards away two Great Pyrenees sheep dogs were on the hunt for coyotes. These dogs are raised with sheep. They fend for themselves and think they are sheep, I'm told. A coyote jumped out of the brush in front of them and took off down into the timber with one dog on his tail. About twenty seconds later there was a loud screeching, "Yeeiahowe." Dog: one, coyote; zero.

The other dog kept jumping around in the thick brush, apparently scent trailing the coyote that had just run past me. In some panic I prepared to encounter the dog, not knowing how I might be greeted. But their hunt was over and it was ok. Another year, I had taken my son Steve and his friend into the same area. The same area Steve and I had "discovered" in 1985. It is a good area, a bit remote and I have seen lots of elk there. Again we ran into a herd of these domestic sheep with two or three of these Great Pyrenees dogs. They are about the size of wolves, huge mouths with long vanilla colored coats, handsome but scary looking. This time we were out in the open and the sheep fed past us at about sixty yards. Here came the dogs. I told my companions, "prepare to defend yourselves." The dogs lowered their heads, stayed between us and the sheep and gave us the look, "don't come one step closer."

September, 2001 I backpacked too much equipment, as usual, up to about eleven thousand feet on "Mystery Mountain" about five miles north of where I usually hunted. The first day I was tired and after getting into a good camping spot I sit down to eat lunch out of the little stainless pot I sometimes take. I watched a large park, maybe ½ mile across and two miles long. I could hear sheep bleating at times way off to the south.

39

I had my tiny radio ear pods in and was engrossed in the news and lunch. All at once I heard, right next to my ear, "ahh, ahh, ahh." First thought, "you're dead!" Second thought, "well, if he wanted me I'd already be dead!" I looked two feet to my left and here was one of those huge dogs panting and sitting next to me. I said in a somewhat shaky voice, "well hello, fella". The dog gave me an, "Im so glad to meet you greeting". Panting without moving.

My education about these two dogs then began in earnest. There was another a male. The one next to me was a female. The male never came closer than twenty yards. I offered them some jerky which they declined. Apparently they are taught not to accept food. I have no idea what they eat, maybe ground squirrels. Perhaps the herders feed them. We kind of socialized a few minutes. I talked to them but did not try to pet or approach very closely. Two feet was plenty close. The female finally did pick up the jerky I had thrown on the ground. After about ½ hour the male stood up and looked at me and said in dog body language, "I'm going to get you some elk." You know, one of those hunches. I thought, "oh yeah sure." The female stayed beside me. The male trotted off into some timber to the southeast. About fifteen minutes later I heard the sound of thundering hooves coming my way from the southeast. Here came five cow elk about twenty yards out and past my camp. My bow was on the ground. I managed to get it up and ready to draw just as the last cow stopped and looked me in the eye at twenty-five yards. Then she was gone with the rest.

I thought, "next time a dog and God tell you something, listen," Ten minutes later the male Pyrenees wandered into camp and said in dog body language, "I thought you were an elk hunter?!"

The dogs fell into a sound sleep. About 4:30 I got ready for the evening's hunt thinking, "They will get up and leave now." They never heard me go. When I got back about dark they were gone. During the nights up there I could hear elk bugling and then the dogs would bark back until very late. I still would not approach these noble dogs, especially when near their sheep, but what an experience.

ELK SQUIRRELS

What do "Elk Squirrels" look like? Well Elk Squirrels are about fifteen inches long counting the tail. They are three shades of a greyed brown in Colorado. They weigh maybe two pounds. They climb the spruce trees during the Fall and throw cones to the forest floor by the dozens. When these furry little friends hit a dead fall log with one of their missiles the sound is almost identical to the sound an elk's hoof makes on the same log. However when you hear an elk's hoof you'll know the difference. Get ready. "Elk Squirrels" are technically know as Pine Squirrels or Chickeree. They get with it at sunrise and chatter loudly to let other squirrels know they aren't welcome. The thumping of cones hitting the ground is usually accompanied by their singing: chattering. The sound an elk's hoof makes is hard to describe but if you can imagine, it has the sound sort of like a very large fingernail or "plastic" thumping either the ground or a log. Get ready!

FOOLING THEIR NOSES

Over the years I've had my doubts about the facts of scent. Seeing deer and elk absolutely go berserk when getting a whiff of myself should have been a good clue. I always tried to keep downwind with varied success. At times I've shot elk with a bow as close as three feet. More recently I've discovered scent hiding clothing, electric blocking clothing, scent subduing liquids, bicarbonate of soda, etc. and cover scents ARE effective tools for hiding yourself. In shooting a bull recently with a bow at close range, elk were all around me for maybe an hour within as close as twenty yards. Partly due to luck and partly due to judicious use of scent hiding clothing and various scent powders, etc. most of them never had a clue. In my opinion bicarbonate of soda is very effective. I carry it in an old clean sock inside a zip lock bag. You can take it out of the bag and bang it all over yourself and equipment making a cloud of scent killing soda all around yourself.

NOTE: I've seen deer and elk go all kinds of directions when traveling. The idea that they always go up wind seems to not be true. One rule however I've noted as an absolute fact is that when spooked they ALWAYS turn immediately into the wind and on to a trail they are familiar with as soon as possible. Their noses always keep them tuned into what is in that direction.

STILL HUNTING

Opening morning of rifle season in central Wisconsin Thanksgiving 1970, I was hunting the edge of a marsh where I had shot at a buck running through willows two weeks before with a bow. I had recently read of a hunter who watched a Whitetail buck get down on its' belly like a mud Marine and crawl into cover between two other hunters. This was news to me that they would act like that. Armed with this knowledge, I was determined to take my time. I felt a six point buck I had missed two weeks prior with a bow might be bedded in the same area. The area I could hunt was only five-hundred yards long on this property edge. I spent an hour going a hundred yards. A light snow drifted from the south from a leaden sky so I could keep great track of wind direction. I was comfortably dressed and the wind was light. The temperature was around twenty -five above.

As I neared the corner of where I could hunt and into the willows where there are deer beds, I slowed down from about a creep to almost standing, even backing up a bit. Standing there for maybe five minutes. Suddenly out of the two foot high marsh grass the buck jumped up within ten feet of me and bounded to the northwest. I brought the 06 scope down on his withers on the second bounce and down he went. DOA. On examination I found my arrow of two weeks previous had clipped his back left knee. The slight wound was well healed. Learn something from every animal you see.

I have enjoyed using the still hunting technique on elk with limited success over the years. It is the most intense way to hunt and mentally exhausting. A book with a great treatment of the how to of still hunting is Advanced Hunting on Deer and Elk Trails by Francis E. Sells, available on amazon.com, used but out of print. This is the best reading on hunting I've ever read. After shooting my first bull in 1958 I decided I wanted to know more of what I was doing. This book led me to another successful hunt the next year. Most hunters walk way too fast. A friend in 1958 who had given up hunting for philosophical reasons but who loves the outdoors introduced me to a method of hunting then, which is similar to still hunting, which took me several years to fully appreciate and use.

Previously my method or non- method was always to go as fast and far as possible in any one day. Full tilt over hill and dale in a straight line. Again, most hunters walk way too fast. Now I ask myself, "What are you doing now? Cruising, hiking, moseying, still hunting, what are you doing now?" I find it much more enjoyable and fulfilling.

My friend showed me after climbing up from Highway 6 in Clear Creek Canyon west of Golden, Colorado how to "be invisible" in the forest. The method is similar to still hunting. Basically you walk very slowly when in cover. Walk maybe two or three steps and than stand still for a few moments or even minutes. The first time he showed me this, we took maybe one half hour to walk one hundred yards. It is similar to being on stand. You take plenty of time looking, with binoculars at times, and listening. When in the open you walk gently across it as being in the open you are going to be easily seen any ways.

If you have made that first scouting trip, watched elk in a relaxed summer situation and come to know the area you are hunting you can be more confident. You don't want to NOW bust through the woods in ignorance. You know the trails now. You know the terrain and where you might happen on your prize. Take it easy, listen, watch, think, smell. Go get 'em but slowly.

Notes:

ATTITUDE

OK, hopefully you've made a scouting trip. You have practiced with the bow or rifle and feel competent. You have zeroed in on at least two good spots to hunt. You get back on the mountain, hunt three days and they aren't there. Now what? Why aren't they here? Good question. A question we don't always have the answer for. I asked a game warden, "where do they go?" He replied, "About 1 ½ miles beyond where you are willing to go." Hopefully you don't have this problem but in fact about 50% of the time you will, hunting on public lands with other hunters.

Quick start answer: go further or move to another area. Remember it's hunting not shopping. If you need guaranteed meat, go to the market, "where no animals were killed!" :-)   It's a lot cheaper unless you are an unusual hunter and consistently successful. Or get a "KBAS deer". "KBAS: Killed By A Speeder" or "Killed by a Semi." Bucks, does, fawns legal year around, no closed season. Comes usually already dead, tenderized and sometimes gutted.

Tongue in cheek of course but seriously; see your sheriff or highway authorities for details. In Colorado they will write you a Road Kill Permit if you wish to pick up the cheapest venison possible. Note to speeders: a taxidermist locally told me that each year over 720 deer are killed by traffic on Highways 50 and 285 between my home town of Cotopaxi and Buena Vista, Colorado. I picked up a small buck a few years ago near here. The Deputy told me that it was the twelfth deer he had dealt with that morning by 11 am. DOH, "dead on the highway."

Back to the subject; Maintaining a positive attitude when the elk have disappeared is one of the toughest things about elk hunting. Some years are better than others of course. 2006 I found elk wherever I went. (In three different units). In 2007 I was very tired from a recent expedition in north west Alaska and didn't hunt real hard so never saw any during bow season. In rifle season a few weeks later I saw two spikes which were not legal. 2008 I never saw one. Back in the in the 50s and 60s I hunted with a crack shot from Wisconsin in Colorado who hunted elk eight years and never got an elk. Sometimes to take a break, go to town and get a shower and spend a night in a motel will do wonders. It can become a battle in the mind, especially if the weather is rough. Elk hunting is mentally taxing. If you have a hunting buddy that helps.

45

WHICH WAY DID THEY GO?

WHY DO ELK DISAPPEAR?

Probably the biggest reason is human pressure. Elk equate gunfire many times with lightning which they hear all their lives. Let them see or smell you however and the panic is on.

OVERCROWDING

One area I've hunted since about 1968 is a fabulous area. A south east facing slope of maybe fifteen square miles, deep with herbage, lots of aspens and fir, cut with many sub ridges. My Father-in-law and I hunted it for many years. It was "discovered" by hunters taking in their friends and those friends taking in their friends, etc. By 1969 it was hunted very heavily by rifle . That year I killed a five point bull with the "Meat Wagon" at 7:15 first morning. I was beginning to learn that if you didn't get your game by 9 am opening morning you weren't going to get one.

I had walked and climbed to a point along a ridge between two gullies in mixed timber. At 7:15 I heard hooves on rocks on a trail just fifteen yards below. As I stood up a five point bull emerged from the gully to the left. He whirled down hill and plunged down the gully. At about fifty yards I got the cross hairs of the "Meat Wagon" on his brain and blam! DOA. Dead on Arrival!

Before shooting my bull I watched as twenty-two jeeps full of hunters growled and climbed their way up the mountain towards me. By 9:15 that morning I had seen forty-nine other hunters. I made a decision that day to get serious about bow hunting. If I wished to be in a crowd I'd go to football games. Pop and I hunted this area together for maybe ten years, mostly with bows. We enjoyed many an elk encounter.

Hunting in Colorado has changed a lot since those days. The seasons are spread out and you see fewer other hunters, normally. The hunting is superior to the past. The herds are bigger. Some areas sport bigger and more bulls. It is far better in many ways. These are the GOOD OL' DAYS of elk hunting in Colorado!

If you aren't there you can't shoot 'em! I take a paperback book and maybe an electric chess set for idle times as I normally hunt alone. It helps.

46

Stupidity

Back to this secret area. One of the last times I hunted there I met a guy who said, "We were in here all last week calling and shooting them with blunts before season, now we can't find them." If I would have used the words on him I was thinking we no doubt would have had a major altercation. I reported him. I had been in the area in June and had seen numerous elk including a herd of about fifty.

Not only is shooting elk out of season with blunts illegal, it is STUPID! Events like this you can't do much about at the moment. You can report the criminal activity to the Game and Fish Department and hope it reduces such insanity in the future.

In the same spot in a later year the second morning of bow season some yahoo was walking all over the woods yelling for his friend, "Al, are you up here?" Like I said, "Stupidity."

They travel

Weather can cause elk hunting to become difficult, especially very dry weather. Try to find their sign near water in any case. Sometimes you just can't figure out why they aren't there. A friend who does not hunt told me of a herd he saw many times here in central Colorado which would make a seventeen mile one way trip to water every evening. Sure enough there is a road sign on the highway warning of elk crossing.

Elk can travel great distances in a hurry. I'm aware of one herd that migrates thirty miles south according to game biologists. They apparently do this in a hurry once they get going. Again, it's called hunting. Thirty miles, to as large and powerful animal as this on their trails is no big deal. Some of these instances I've noted are exceptional and negative. During about 70% of my elk hunts I've found elk where they are supposed to be.

Livestock

Again: a hunter I met in 2008, e-mailed me that he went up the last weekend of bow season. The bulls were bugling all over the place. Saturday morning cowboys came in to round up their cattle out of the National Forest. They rode all over the place and the elk disappeared. You would hope they would be considerate and do their roundups between seasons. It is multiple use land however. I wish I could reserve it to myself but such is life. Your own "private" hunting spots must be shared with others. One option if something like this happens is to go somewhere else or return a week or so later. Perhaps conditions will have changed.

Predators

Lions, bears, coyotes, and now again wolves are in the forests 24/7/365 with elk. Bears are more prevalent thanks to tree huggers getting spring bear season closed. Elk live with these animals night and day and if, particularly lions and bears are currently working your choice hunting spot elk may move. A lion can take down a full grown bull elk and elk respect and fear them. Bears routinely kill elk calves and know exactly when and where to find them. Coyotes are not normally an issue due to their smaller size. Elk will chase them off. My dog Grizzly Bear was chased twice by a bull, then a cow elk while we were summer scouting.

SOLUTIONS THAT HAVE WORKED FOR ME

One solution is to move on to another area. Perhaps that area may not be very far. 1985 my son Steve and I had driven high up in the heavy snow the day before rifle season at about eleven thousand feet altitude and were not finding sign.

After a couple days poking around and still not finding anything we drove down the canyon, somewhat in despair. Fortunately there was fresh snow and a couple miles below we saw elk tracks from the car, crossing the road and up hill to the north. That led to the discovery of not only elk on that trip but in examining other approaches to the terrain in later years, good hunting in a heavily hunted unit. It's become one of my honey holes. Sometimes just hiking a bit further and keeping on looking for good sign will pan out.

I was not finding elk in this area on a hunt in 2001. On visiting with another hunter I learned he planned to ride in on horseback further in to the north. Thinking that over and not wanting to disturb his hunt I drove about sixty miles around the other end of the mountain and hiked in from the north. I landed in elk paradise. They were bugling and I had nine bulls going one evening. We were screaming back and forth across eight hundred yards of a high timberline park at each other, but they would not, after an hour of this, come over to be shot. But what fun! Thus began several more years of trying to put the sneak on them in this new spot.

In thinking back over our 1985 hunt, the reason we did not find elk at first was that we were too high. We had literally dug through snow banks on the road to get up to about eleven thousand feet altitude. We camped on the ground in snow and walked around in blizzard conditions for two days, no sign at all "duh?" The elk were below us due to the heavy snow. Once we drove down to a lower altitude and as I said cut sign in the snow we had a clue as to were to go.

"Hunter's snow" is truly a God send! Anything up to about a foot you can get around in and it makes tracking a dream! In 2002 I got into a new spot in the Gore Range. It snowed some days about three inches. Perfect! On the third day I cut the tracks of two cow elk and followed them for maybe three hours and four miles. About eleven in the morning I caught up with them. With the rifle at the ready for the past forty-five minutes I finally spotted them. I quickly knelt next to a small fir for rest and at seventy-five yards put the cross-hairs on the one I could see well enough. One shot and off she ran to pile up in about thirty-five yards.

After dressing her out and dividing the meat into back packable chunks I set off back to the truck. Dark came early in October and after about a half hour I got lost. It was snowing. I was new to a GPS and in trying to short cut my way got into some real tough stuff. About 9pm after trying to cross a beaver dam on thin ice I climbed back up a steep slick bank. My flashlight was dying. In the dark blowing snow but with some occasional moonlight I could see the game trail had dark objects across it.

On close examination when the flashlight brightened a bit I could see that they were not all logs. Some were "beaver mines" cutting up the bank and were up to six feet deep. I realized I was going to break a leg if I kept going so I arranged my clothes as best I could for the cold and laid down in the trail to try and sleep. I put the meat down for a pillow and a large black plastic bag over my feet and cut a hole for my head in another. I had a great "super suit", I call it, on as well and some hand

49

warmers. The cold would wake me every once in a while but I actually slept most of the night until daylight when I could see well. When I looked at the beaver's mines or actually trenches in the pond bank I was very glad I'd stopped. I got back to the truck the next day and until about 1 am the next snowy morning I packed the remaining two loads of meat out. A perfect "hunter's snow" led me straight to elk I would not have seen otherwise.

The "early itch" once again!

Some hunters are apparently just up out of the city. They may have been "penned up" in an office job, busy, cooling their heels on the freeway log jams, etc. They don't get into the mountains often or "something". They get to the hills a day or two early so they roar around on their ATVs, target practice, and walk the woods to see what the prospects are. You can count on it; the elk take off and opening morning they are nowhere to be seen. I've made it a practice to find places where this doesn't happen. One area I like is in one of those summer concentrations. Often, even during rifle season I've seen only three or four other hunters in there. However for one or two seasons during bow season I encountered "hunters" or so you would guess, tooling around on ATVs, illegally going past, around, and over Forest Service barricades and signs declaring, "No vehicles past this." I complained to the Forest Service as did others and they dropped a half mile of trees across that access and even the thick headed can't ruin the area. The last time I was in there I saw no other hunters. They were able to go up another route to the west to other spots and leave the elk bedding areas undisturbed. Great!

More stupidity

In this same spot one year some guys drove all over, off trail, through the parks and meadows on ATVs loudly talking as they drove right through elk bedding areas, repeatedly, oblivious to real hunting, apparently. There are several major elk trails through this meadow. The Forest Service and BLM have taken measures such as previously written here to curb such nonsense nation wide.

I'm reminded of my Dad telling me about a meeting at which he was a speaker. He was a designer of heavy equipment and part of his job was to present new machinery and teach dealers how to utilize them. In this meeting a guy stood up and asked him, "French, why don't you invent the fool proof machine?" Dad said, "I did that once and they just kept trying out new fools on me."

We all do dumb things at times. I certainly have. Maybe some of these examples will help you to be more successful as a hunter and keep your own foolishness down to a minimum. We can do little to change the behavior of others. Elk will soon leave an area for quite some time if they are subjected to very much of such nonsense. The idea, even if you are just "summer scouting" is to be there without being obvious.

Be quiet. I have seen elk in the above mentioned park many times and shot them there. Old logging roads are great for walk in access but if they are legally closed to vehicles, park it and walk or you're hurting your own chances as well as making some "unfriendlies."

Notes

HOW ELK HUNTING
HAS CHANGED

Again a lot has been learned by hunters since the 1950s. A very few guys used to call using a whistle sometimes made out of plastic or aluminum pipe. Calling has become much more sophisticated especially in the past twenty years and it's hard to tell another hunter from an elk at times. Calls are far superior to what they were in the past. Clothing is vastly better. Instead of red or pink silk like "alert" vests we have really bright orange flourescent clothing. Modern hunting clothes don't "ZIP" their way through the brush scaring the daylights out of everything for four hundred yards. Everything is superior. We could not even think of a device that told you exactly where you were, give you live weather, show satellite, aerials and live radio from outer space. "What in the world is a satellite?' We would have asked. A lot is vastly superior. However some things never change. Elk for example are the same. One controversial thing which is different which I like is that Congress passed laws back in the 1970s or 80s making some National Forest areas; Wilderness. We used to drive jeeps way up in what is now Wilderness. You could drive ALL over and people did. The result was that it was like a circus. You might be setting on stand waiting for game to come by and kids on cycles would charge past, repeatedly. I'm glad there are other areas for those activities now but in the past it was a real circus and a recipe for personal violence over these issues as well. The elk have a refuge where the only way to them in some areas is on foot or horse back. Even the Forest Service cannot land helicopters in Wilderness.

Again: These are the "Good Old Days" of Elk hunting. Back about 1890 elk as well as all other wildlife were in grave danger of becoming extinct. elk, deer, bear; the "works" were served in restaurants through out the west as civilization moved to the Pacific shore.

It is estimated that only four hundred elk survived in all of Colorado and only in the northern mountains by 1890. Alarmed hunters and conservationists pressed for laws outlawing elk hunting for the next fifty years. Elk were trucked in from Yellowstone. By 1939 a season was allowed. My Grandfather and Dad began to hunt them in those days. At this writing nearly eighty years later, in Colorado you can purchase TWO elk licenses. **Again these are the "good old days" of elk hunting in Colorado.** Enjoy and appreciate that.

Notes

MEAN ELK

A friend of mine near here ran a small zoo. He had bears, African lions, cougars, fox, etc. He had a bull elk which he hand raised. It was a pet. One September day during the rut because he was so familiar with the bull he didn't pay it much attention as he was cleaning it's pen and feeding him. The bull charged him and got him down against the fence. It gored him and was killing him. His wife ran into the house and came back and killed the elk with a .22 rifle shot to the back of it's head. My friend spent several weeks in the hospital. A bull elk's whole attitude radically changes due to increased testosterone in his system during the rut.

This bull, in the Stone Mountain Zoo near Atlanta, Georgia tried to climb the fence after me. He had my "undivided" attention! He was hissing like a large snake. If he could have spoken English he would have said, "I know what you've been doing!"

ELK CAN BE DANGEROUS

I don't want to overstate the issue but they are very large animals. Cows will take you in the spring if you get near their calves, especially in a national park setting. The Denver Zoo back in 1960 had a very substantial bull. He probably weighed one thousand pounds. Dad's skeet champion friend had helped acquire the bull for the zoo.

One October afternoon I happened to be there. It was cold and windy and I didn't have enough clothing on so decided to jog past the elk's pen which was maybe about an acre in size. The bull had his head to the ground grazing about thirty feet away. As I jogged past he lunged at the hog wire fence, bulging it out about two to three feet. I wondered, "What?" Stopped but then again started to jog on past. Again he charged the fence. I got the message and coldly WALKED on.

About 1986 my wife and I were visiting the Stone Mountain Zoo near Atlanta, Georgia. We were on vacation and I was spending time researching the animals for prospective paintings. It was Fall and the elk's antlers were in fine fiddle. In other words, the rut was on. The fence of their pen wasn't real tall, maybe six feet, not very substantial. Also there was a boardwalk in the bottom part of the pen which took you right past them and the boardwalk was elevated so that you looked the animals right in the eyes. A handsome set up.

The largest bull; a six pointer came down to the fence, visually "zeroed" me, raised his head straight up and hissed, then proceeded to try to climb the fence within just three feet of me. You remember what they say about how animals can tell, right? A couple years later I was able to study what seemed to be the same bull in late summer, about July. He was in velvet and bedded down close to the fence so that I could stand, study and sketch him from just ten feet. While doing this I heard what seemed to be a small bird chirping. The sound was almost continuous. After a while it became evident that the sound was the bull grinding his ivories. Whether in aggravation at me or just tension wasn't apparent but he was glaring. Aren't you glad that normally they are afraid of humans.

Once while my Keeshond, "Grizzly Bear" and I were on a four day summer scouting trip near Crested Butte,

Colorado, we heard elk calling in the alpine meadows to our east. We had seen them above timberline and had busted one on our way from the truck up through the forest to the night's camp. The next morning we put the sneak on them with a camera. I stayed behind a tree, Griz, who looked sort of like a coyote as she was part wolf, walked out into their view after I allowed her. Here came the lead cow on the run to take the dog. When she got within about twenty-five yards I stepped out into their sight and off they ran, bull, cows, and all.

My Father-in-law shot a large bull with a recurve bow at about twenty-five yards one September. Pop was out in the open. The arrow struck the bull in the front leg bone and fell out on the ground. The bull raised his head and glared at Pop who then began to think about tree climbing.

Bulls have picked hunters and artists up in their antlers with deadly intent. Elk, as I've illustrated here can be aggressive. But normally they are terrified of us.

Elk don't like people.

KEEP YOUR SPOTS A SECRET

If you wish to go back to your hard won favorite spot and watch bocoos of other people tramp around just let it slip or blab about your place. I've even caught grandmas scouting for their grand-kids. Again, I learned the hard way to keep my lips zipped. "Loose lips sink ships and ruin hunting spots."

Here are some ways I've learned to deal with this social situation without being too rude. In response to the question, "where do you hunt?" I'll say, "in Colorado" or "in unit humdehum, above a town with no name about twenty-five miles at the end of road zero, on Secret Mountain, at the top of Mystery Creek just under Magic Ridge", or something to that effect. About half way through this little "ditty" they usually crack up and you have avoided an awkward conversation politely. Some guys just stare back at you.

A couple years ago I had packed out a nice bull shot with a bow. I met a guy in camp who asked the usual questions. I told him that, "a hunter who tells where he hunts also writes blank checks to strangers." I thought he was going to choke to death laughing. These statements, thought through before hand allow you to avoid spilling the beans, protect your hard found and thus very expensive hunting haunts and I've never met anyone who didn't enjoy the banter. It's a fun way to say, "I don't tell." Or just say, "I don't tell."

NOTE ON COST OF A GOOD SPOT;
I have spent thousands of dollars and many years discovering many of my spots. At last count I have about twenty-five areas squirreled away. They are not something I give away lightly.

I normally hunt alone. If you are hunting with others, the company can encourage each other in your search. We've all noticed that the first thing many hunters do when they meet other hunters is pump them for information, hoping to find game. I try to avoid this tactic. I feel it is rude and amateurish. On the other hand keeping your ears open isn't a bad idea. Some hunters don't seem to mind sharing some information. I've "ruined" a couple great areas by not following this rule. Since then, "Mum" is the word. During my fourteen years as a Wisconsin resident I

Hunted often in central Wisconsin. I found a great spot and took several Whitetail deer there. I took one friend there and we "kept it to ourselves." One young man begged me to take him. After some thought and being sympathetic towards him I agreed, on the grounds that he would never take anyone else, either go alone or with one of us. The very next weekend we encountered him there with one of his friends.

You learn a lot about a person's character under hunting conditions. Being burned I right there made the policy of not taking anyone else, as a general rule. I found sign in later years that my honey hole was "ruined." I made the mistake of sharing a great spot in Colorado with some very tight lipped hunter "friends" in Wisconsin. About ten years later I read a letter to the editor of Colorado Outdoors from Wisconsin hunters complaining that, "there are too many guys in "blank Park."

ELK MEAT MYTHS AND FACTS AND OPINIONS

I've heard all kinds of statements about venison and what makes for a bad batch. I'm not the expert on this but here's some opinions.

" You've got to get the hide off ASAP." **MY opinion:** the animal has been wearing that hide since before birth. I have been taught and am careful not to get my hands on the scent glands. I'm told there are solutions in the glands that can taint the meat. I believe that. You can smell them. I cut the glands off and throw then aside so they don't come in contact with the meat.

Don't allow the feces or urine to come in contact with the meat. I try hard to keep this from happening. If it does, I immediately wash it off.

"Don't put the meat in plastic bags." My opinion; "as long as the meat is well cooled, the plastic won't hurt." To keep blood out of my backpack I have often placed it in a plastic bag first. My experience is that it doesn't hurt, however if you put it in a hot or warm bag and leave it very long your meat will spoil.

"Get it in cheese cloth bags." My opinion; Probably doesn't hurt but the meat can dry out on the outsides if you don't wet down the cheese cloth from time to time. The dried meat will have to be trimmed off to make a nice cut.

I have found a rule that must not be violated; KEEP THE MEAT CLEAN AND COOL IT ASAP!

Another rule which makes for good tasting venison which isn't always done. I age deer or elk meat for about ten to fourteen days at about thirty-five degrees. I don't let the meat freeze. If conditions outdoors or in a shed, etc., will allow, I've hung it for up to fourteen days.

The experts say that this allows the meat fibers to begin to break up. This makes for a more tender cut. If it isn't aged you pretty well can count on tough steaks.

One exception to this I've experienced was a young Nilgai I shot on the Kenedy Ranch. We ate the back straps and tenderloins barbequed that night and they were like butter.

Maybe you've heard of a hunter who may or may not have gutted the animal then has thrown it on the hot hood and drives a long way home. You can about count on it the meat has been ruined. Meat that has been laid in the dirt is impossible to clean up. Makes for gritty chewing and tough on teeth.

"Do you get your own meat back when you take it to a butcher." I asked a butcher in Wisconsin when I took some deer meat in to be processed into summer sausage. HE just laughed.

Because I've back packed my meat out sometimes miles, I don't want to carry any more weight than absolutely necessary. I took to boning out the animal on the spot, not even gutting it and leaving the hide, entrails, bones, etc. I take all the meat I can cut off the animal. The Colorado Division of Parks and Wildlife offers a booklet that describes how to do this.

Basically I make a cut down the backbone and down each leg and lay the meat on the flayed hide to keep it clean, rolling the animal over using a rope like a block and tackle if needed. Don't forget the tenderloins. You've taken everything you want in the way of meat this way and the coyotes and bears can have the rest. If you wish for the hide, heart, liver, etc., of course you will have to put in more work for those.

My dear wife recently told me that, "you have to get all the sinew off, that's what makes the meat wild." So being ornery I left some sinew on some small cuts from low on the front legs I call, "tidbits." Currently I am eating some of that as an experiment. No wild taste! A friend insists on using a filet knife and cutting all sinew out of the meat, however. His elk meat tastes great.

ELK RANGE AND SUMMER CONCENTRATIONS

Arranged by counties from northwest Colorado down, then to the right and down to the southeastern "elk" counties

The 24 maps are arranged from top to bottom then left to right as you would view a county map of Colorado. Some counties are grouped on one page as they fit. They make no distinction as to public or private land or any legal issues. Know where you are. I have found elk in both, the summer concentrations and summer range. In winter range they are generally found in low land areas closer to civilization after most seasons are closed.

Elk range in Colorado is basically in the western 2/3rds of the state. The maps are intended as a rough "starter" guide and a trip handbook. Only the summer range and concentrations are shown in this book for brevity. Generally elk move down in altitude during heavy snows which usually start in November. They may not be in the areas shown on these maps again until May or June. See Colorado's Division of Parks and Wildlife website for more detailed information.

HOW TO USE THE FOLLOWING MAPS: Coordinate them with Colorado's Parks and Wildlife hunting regulations and topographical maps.

County maps are arranged in a pattern as shown by arrow

These counties not included.

COLORADO

MOFFAT COUNTY

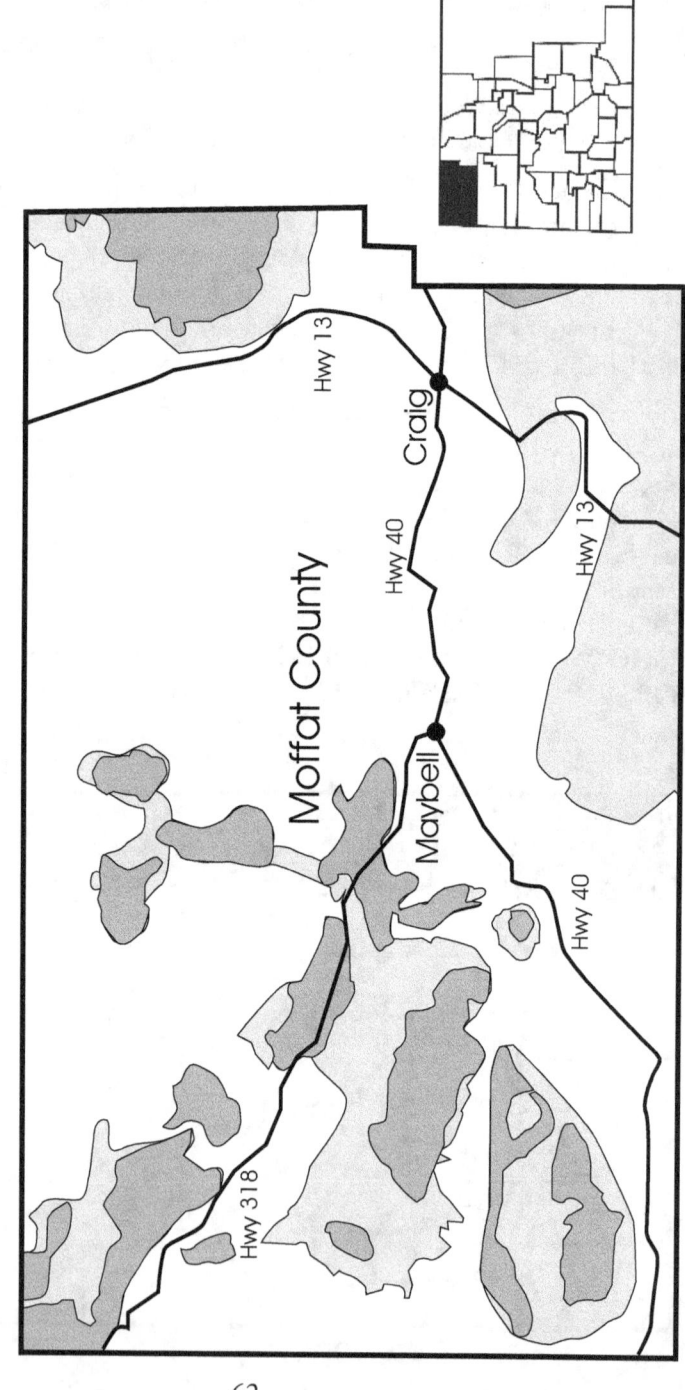

Hwy 13

Craig

Hwy 40

Hwy 13

Moffat County

Maybell

Hwy 40

Hwy 318

RIO BLANCO & GARFIELD COUNTIES

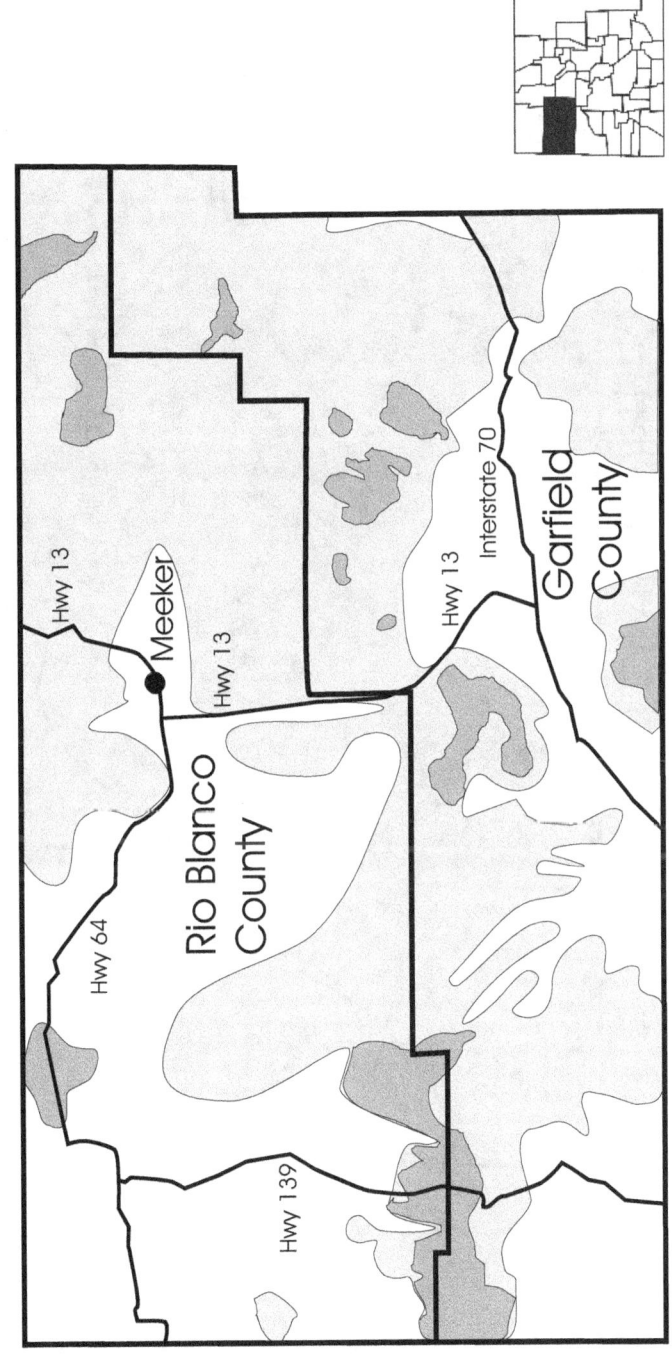

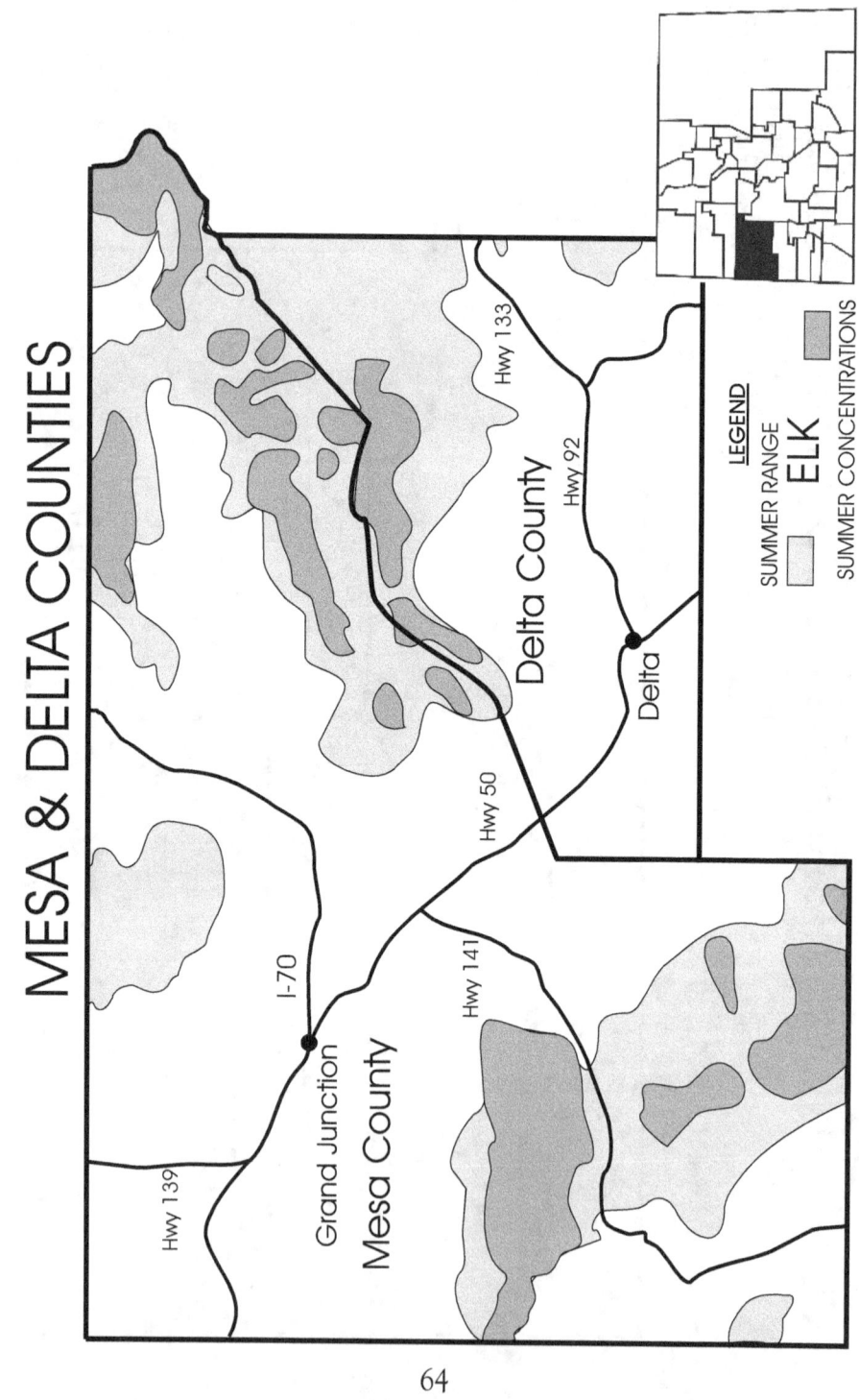

MESA & DELTA COUNTIES

LEGEND

SUMMER RANGE

ELK

SUMMER CONCENTRATIONS

Hwy 133

Hwy 92

Delta County

Delta

Hwy 50

I-70

Hwy 139

Grand Junction

Mesa County

Hwy 141

64

MONTROSE COUNTY

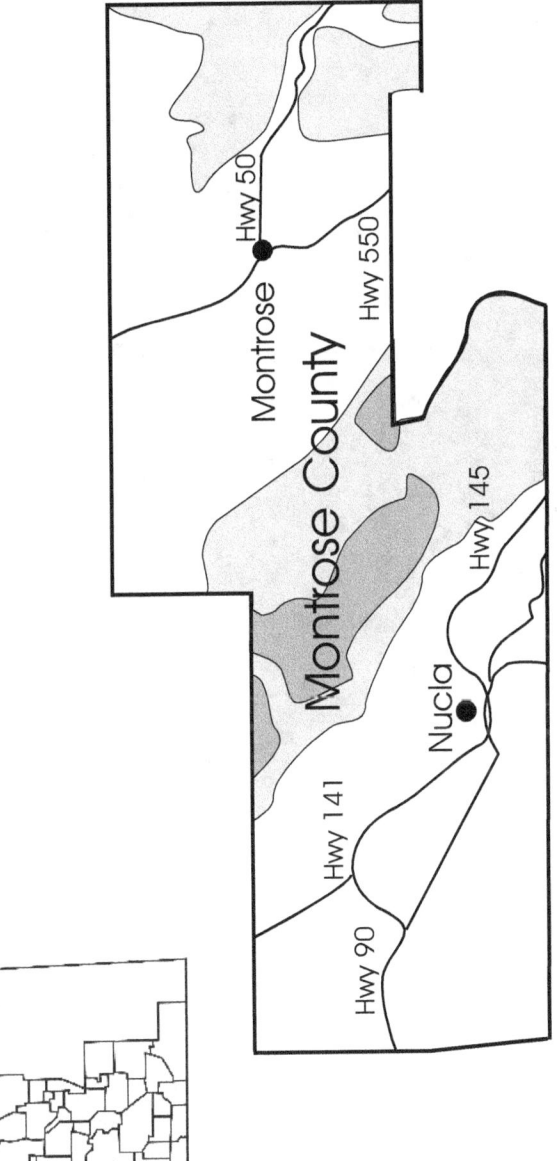

Montrose

Hwy 50

Hwy 550

Montrose County

Hwy 145

Hwy 141

Nucla

Hwy 90

LEGEND

SUMMER RANGE
ELK

SUMMER CONCENTRATIONS

SAN MIGUEL, OURAY, DELORES, & SAN JUAN COUNTIES

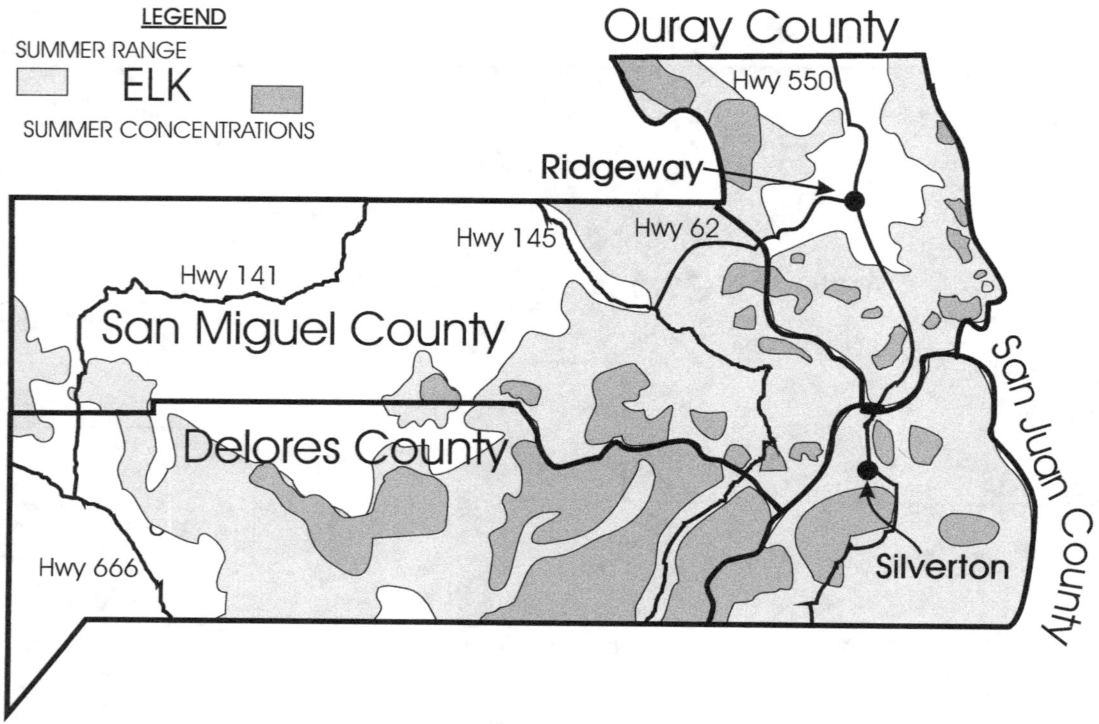

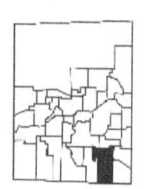

LEGEND

SUMMER RANGE
ELK
SUMMER CONCENTRATIONS

San Juan County

Silverton

Ouray County

Hwy 550

Ridgeway

Hwy 62

Hwy 145

San Miguel County

Delores County

Hwy 141

Hwy 666

66

MONTEZUMA & LA PLATA COUNTIES

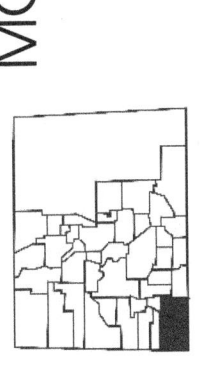

Hwy 550

Durango

Hwy 160

Hwy 160

La Plata County

Hwy 184

Hwy 145

Hwy 140

Montezuma County

Hwy
160
666

Hwy 666

Hwy 160

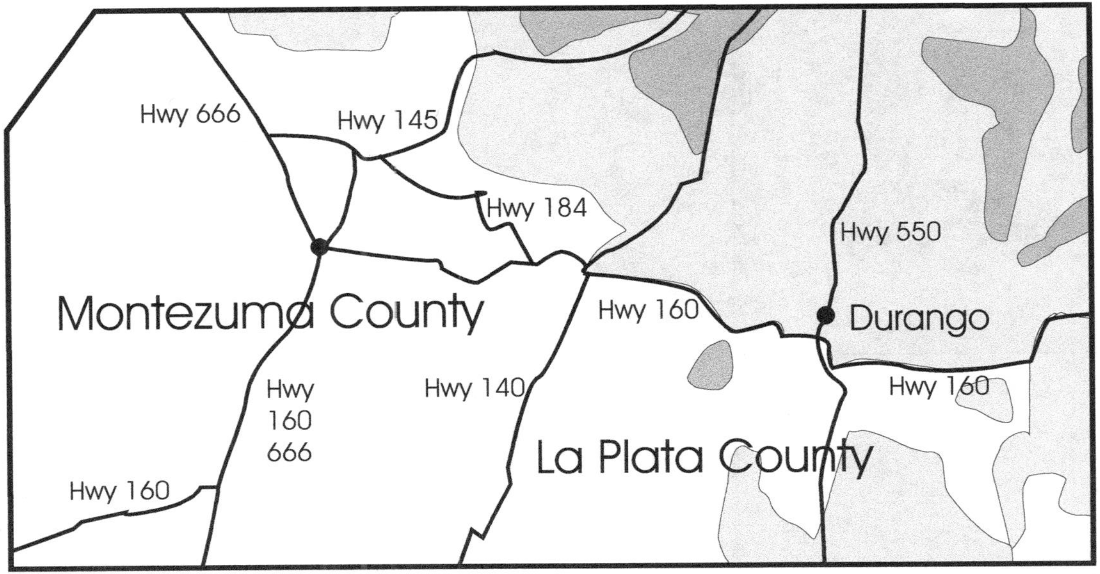

ROUTT COUNTY

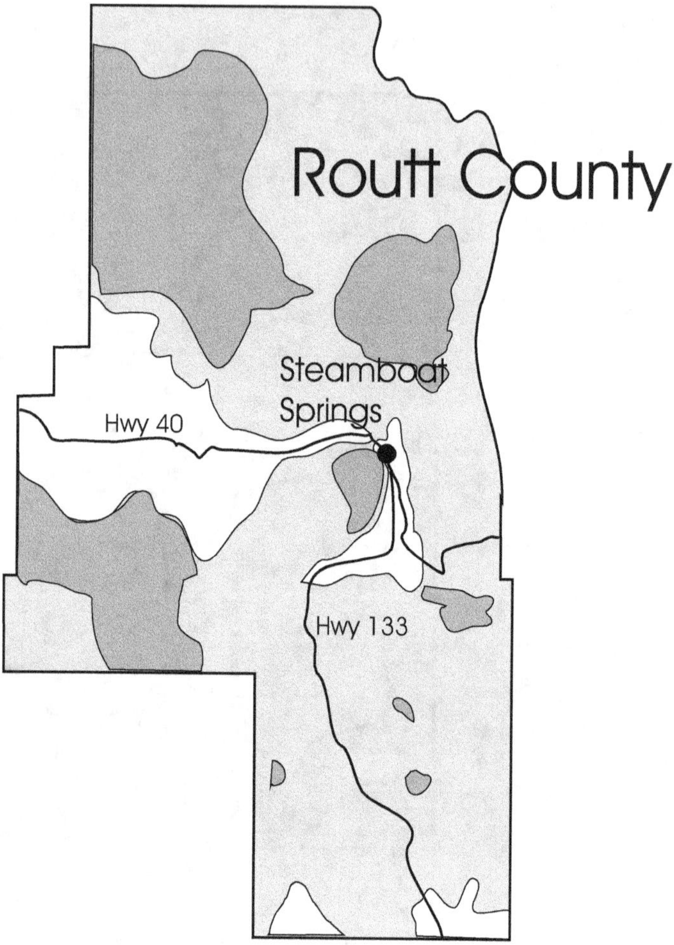

Routt County

Steamboat
Springs

Hwy 40

Hwy 133

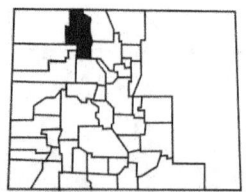

<u>LEGEND</u>

SUMMER RANGE

ELK

SUMMER CONCENTRATIONS

EAGLE & SUMMIT COUNTIES

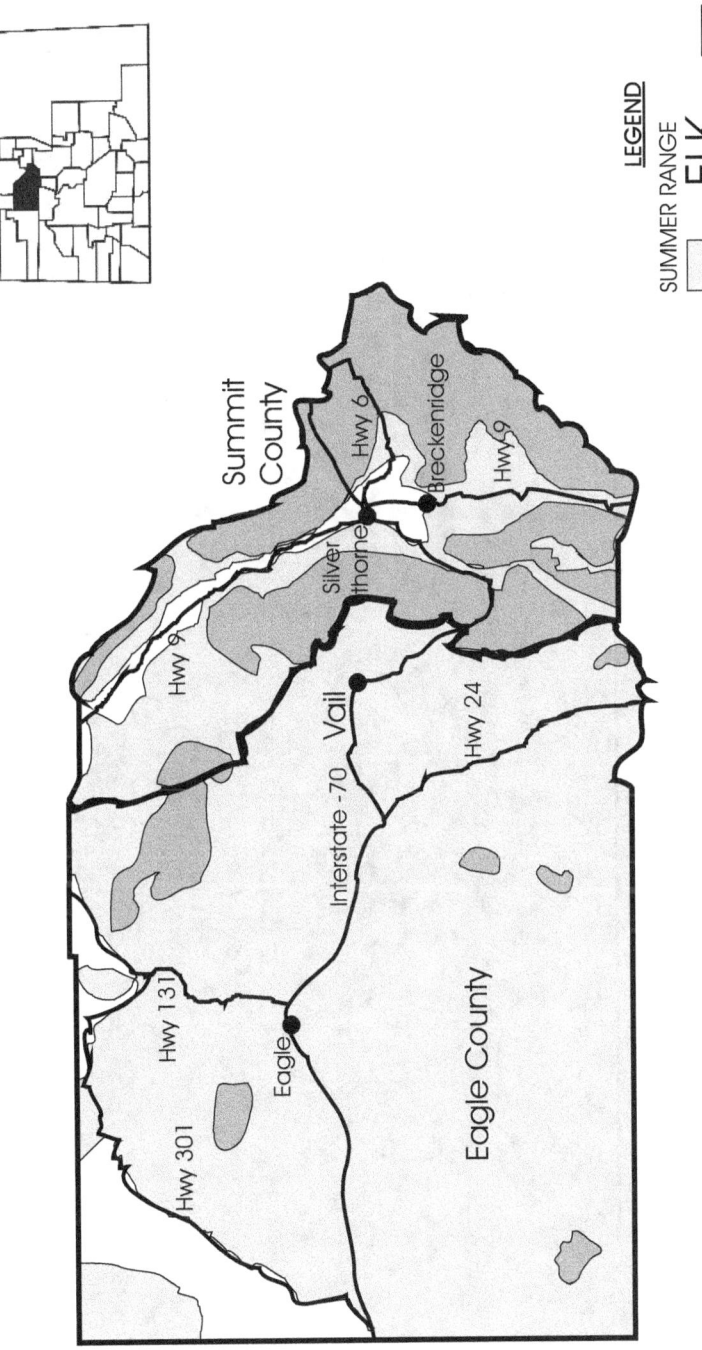

LEGEND

SUMMER RANGE
ELK

SUMMER CONCENTRATIONS

Summit County

Breckenridge

Hwy 6

Hwy 9

Silver thorne

Hwy 9

Vail

Hwy 24

Interstate-70

Hwy 131

Eagle

Hwy 301

Eagle County

PITKIN COUNTY

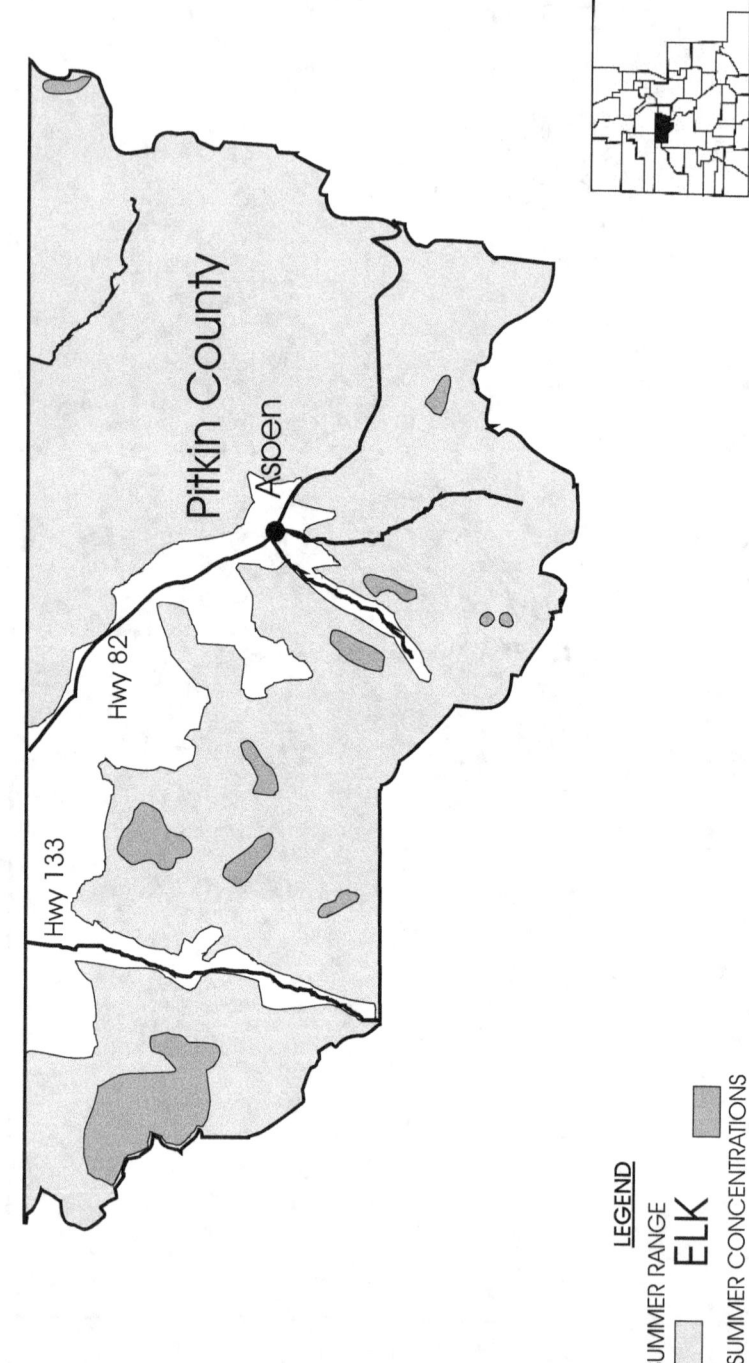

Pitkin County

Pitkin County

Aspen

Hwy 82

Hwy 133

LEGEND

SUMMER RANGE

ELK

SUMMER CONCENTRATIONS

GUNNISON COUNTY

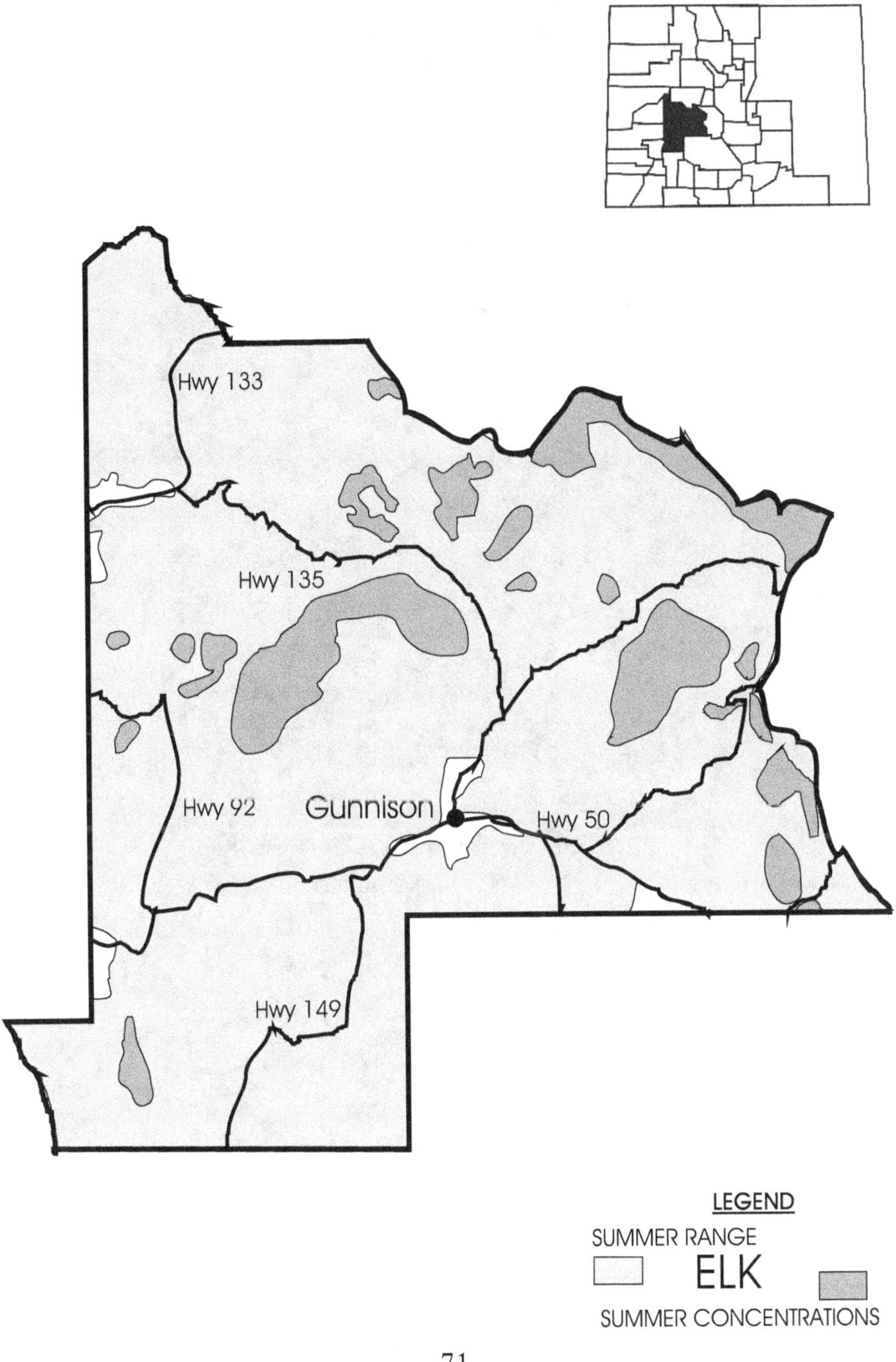

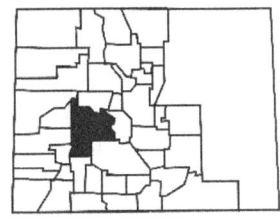

Hwy 133

Hwy 135

Hwy 92

Gunnison

Hwy 50

Hwy 149

LAKE & CHAFFEE COUNTIES

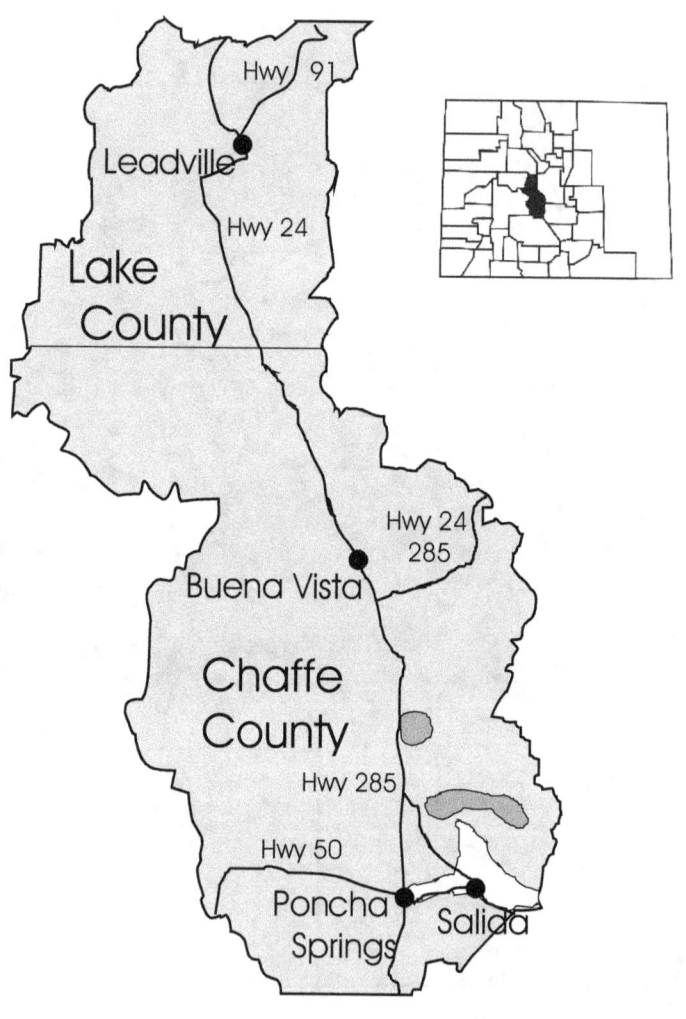

Hwy 91

Leadville

Hwy 24

Lake County

Hwy 24
285

Buena Vista

Chaffe County

Hwy 285

Hwy 50

Poncha Springs

Salida

LEGEND

SUMMER RANGE

ELK

SUMMER CONCENTRATIONS

HINSDALE & MINERAL COUNTIES

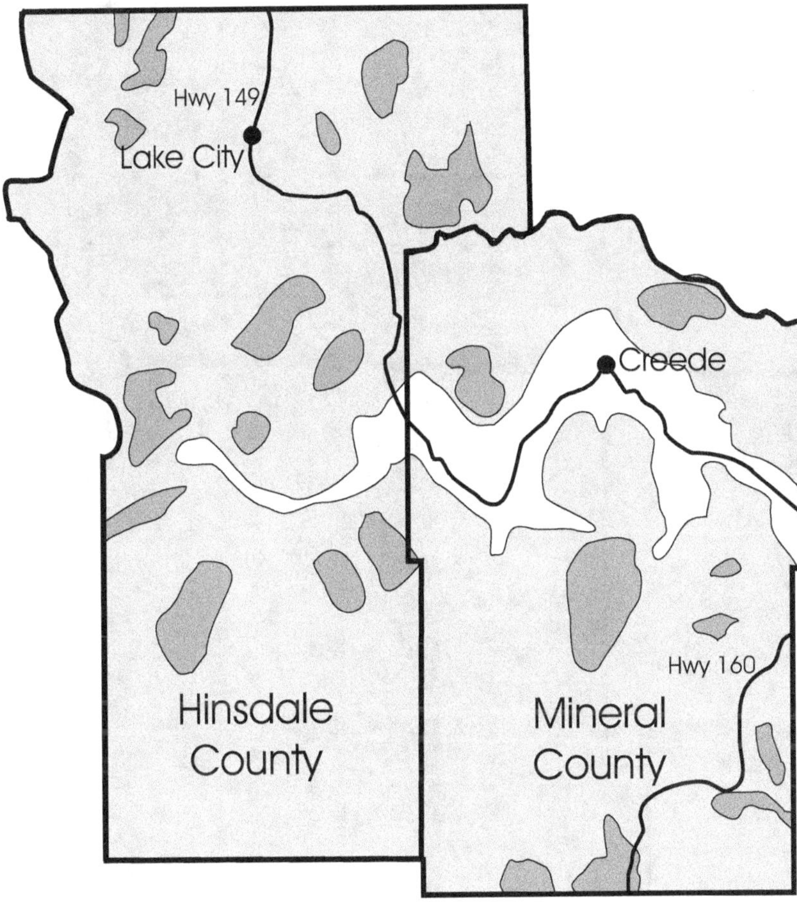

Hwy 149

Lake City

Creede

Hwy 160

Hinsdale
County

Mineral
County

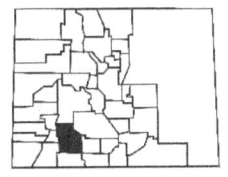

ARCHULETA COUNTY

Hwy 160

Hwy 84

Pagosa Springs

Hwy 160

Hwy 151

JACKSON & GRANDE COUNTIES

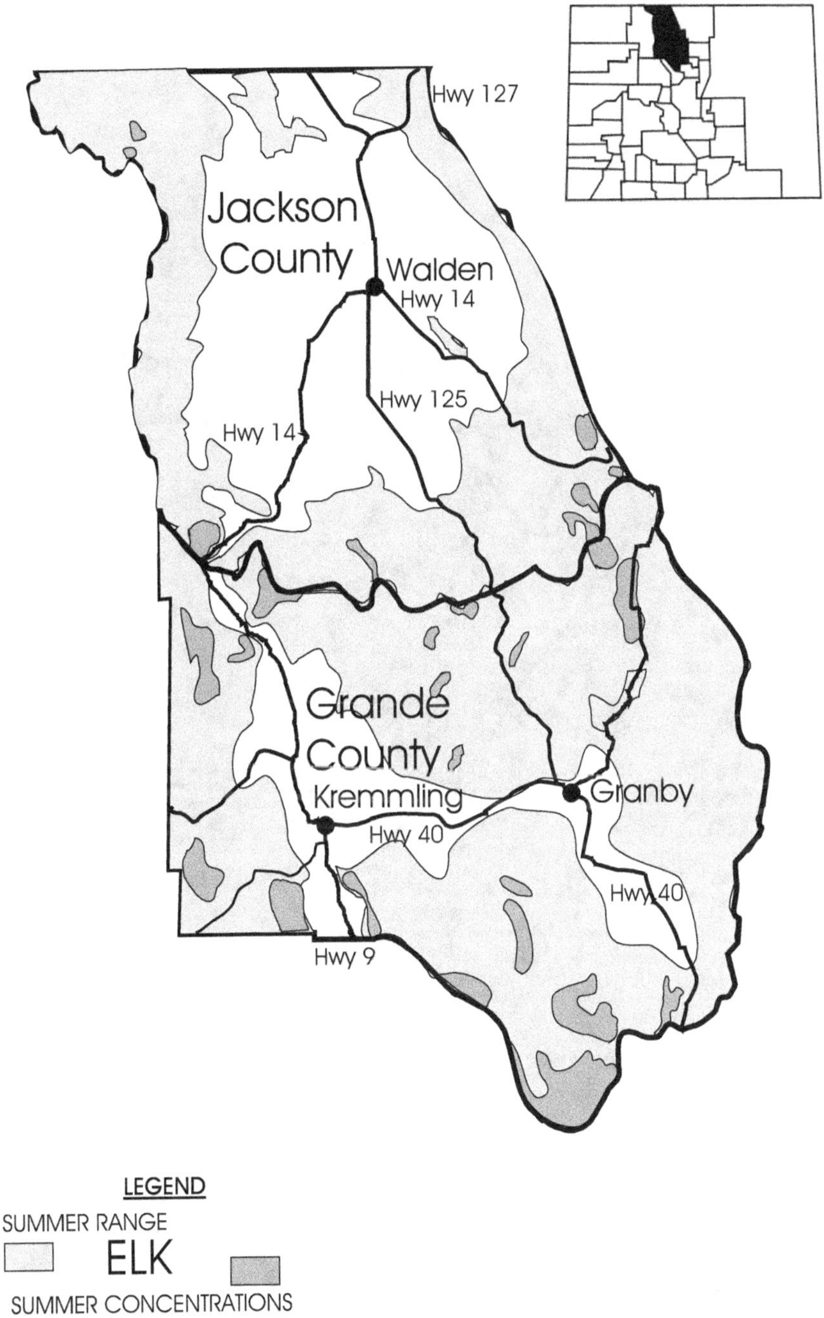

Jackson
County

Walden
Hwy 14

Hwy 127

Hwy 125

Hwy 14

Grande
County

Kremmling

Granby

Hwy 40

Hwy 40

Hwy 9

LEGEND

SUMMER RANGE

 ELK

SUMMER CONCENTRATIONS

PARK COUNTY

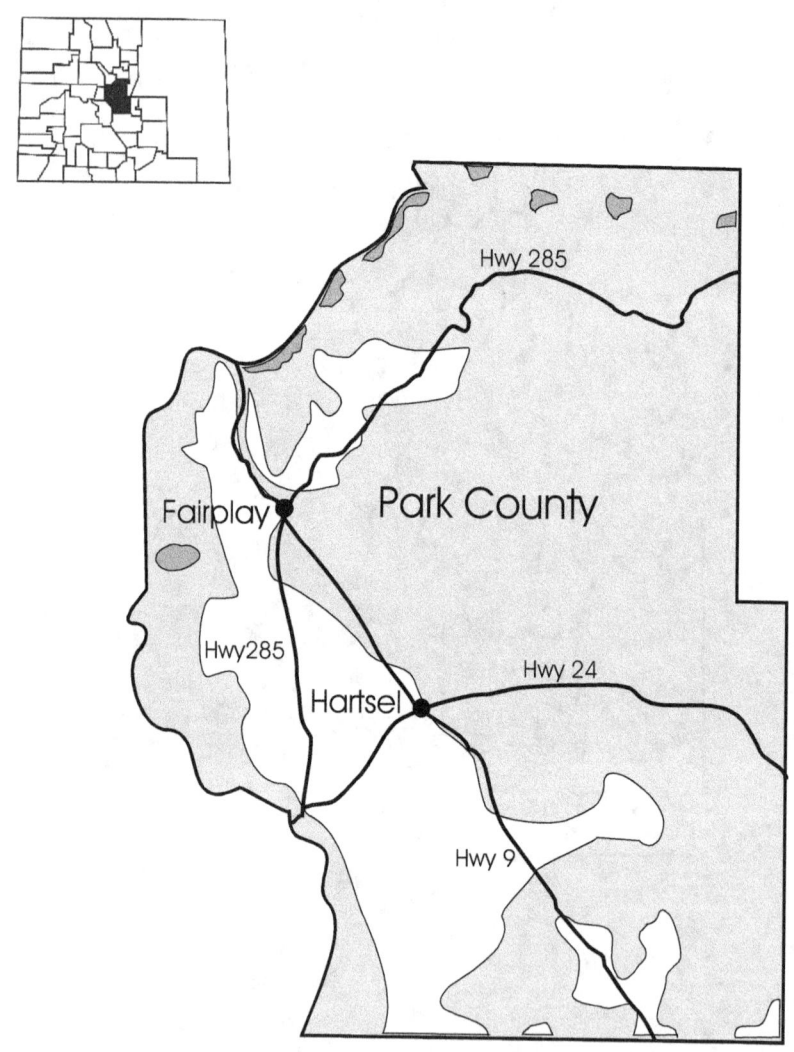

Hwy 285

Park County

Fairplay

Hwy285

Hartsel

Hwy 24

Hwy 9

LEGEND

SUMMER RANGE

ELK

SUMMER CONCENTRATIONS

FREMONT COUNTY

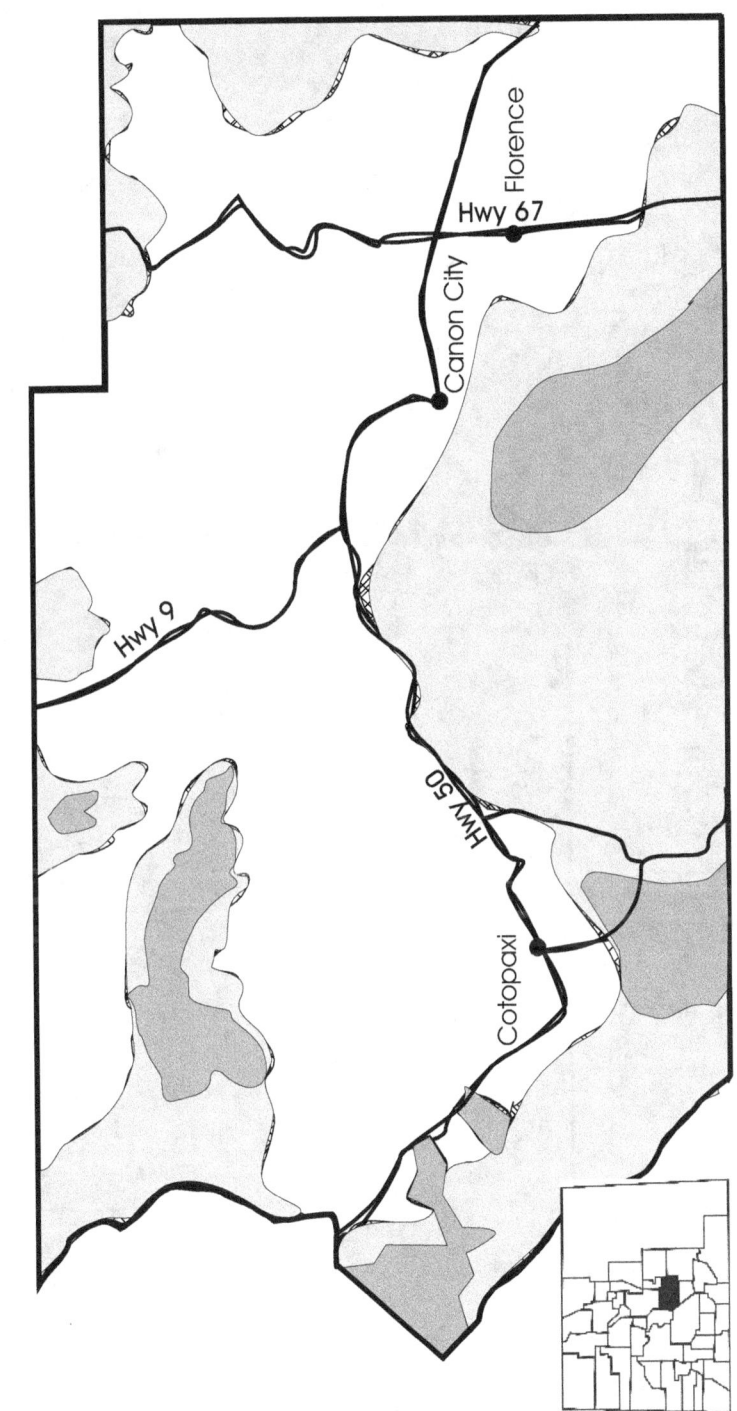

LEGEND

SUMMER RANGE
ELK
SUMMER CONCENTRATIONS

Florence

Hwy 67

Canon City

Hwy 9

Hwy 50

Cotopaxi

SAGUACHE COUNTY

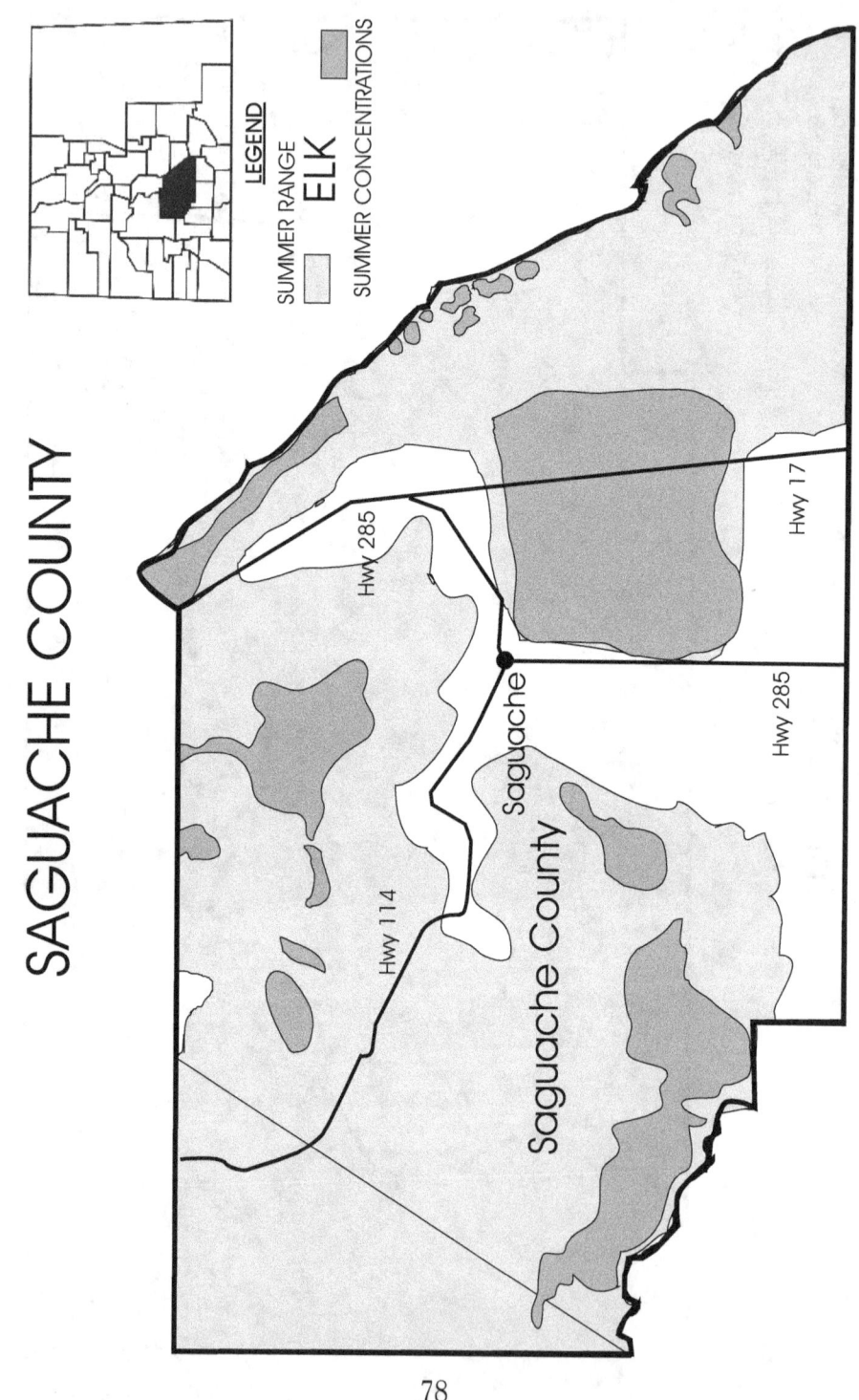

Hwy 285

Hwy 17

Hwy 285

Saguache

Saguache County

Hwy 114

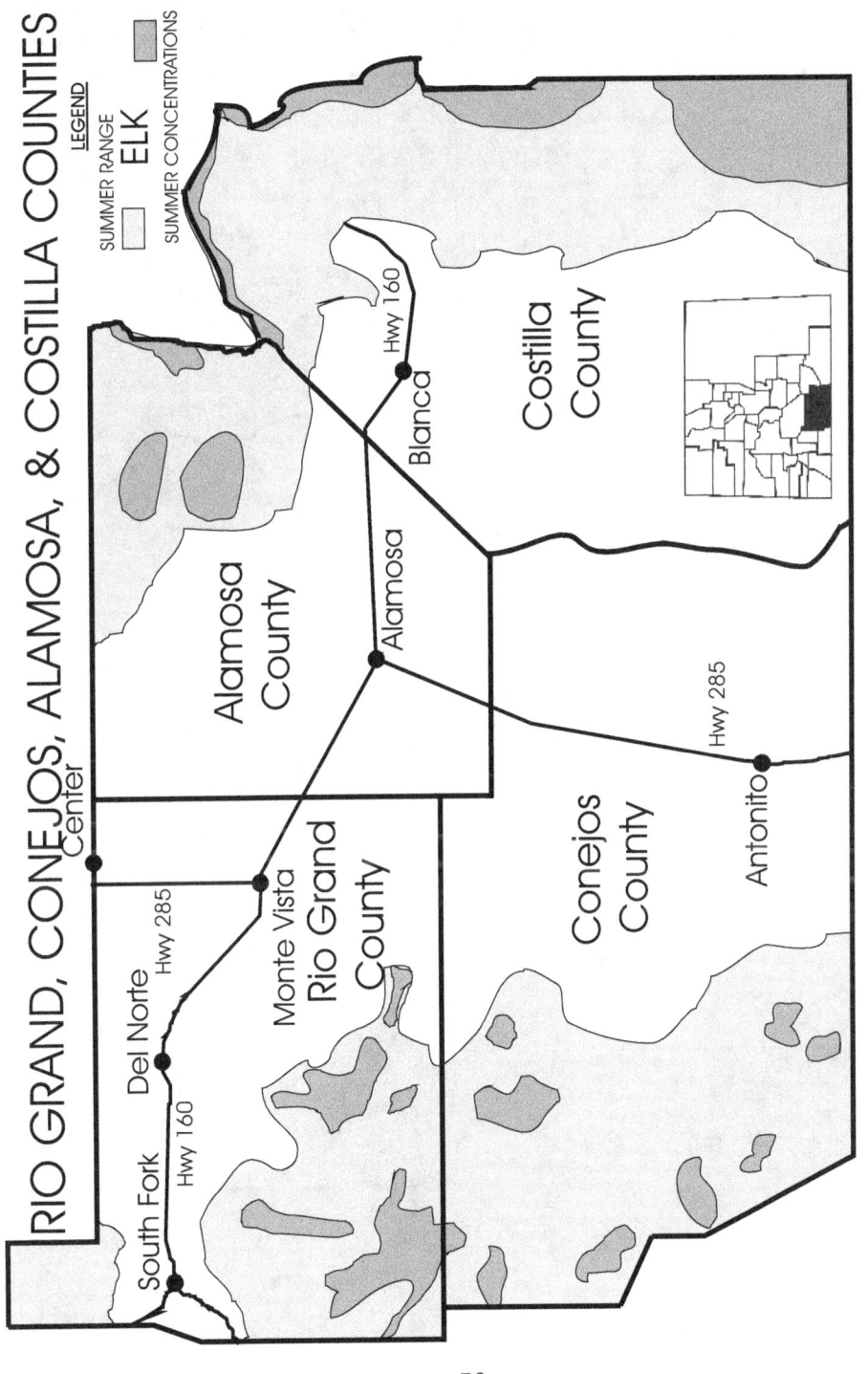

RIO GRAND, CONEJOS, ALAMOSA, & COSTILLA COUNTIES

LEGEND

SUMMER RANGE
ELK
SUMMER CONCENTRATIONS

Alamosa County

Costilla County

Conejos County

Rio Grand County

Center

Blanca

Hwy 160

Alamosa

Hwy 285

Antonito

Monte Vista

Del Norte

Hwy 285

Hwy 160

South Fork

LARIMER & BOULDER COUNTIES

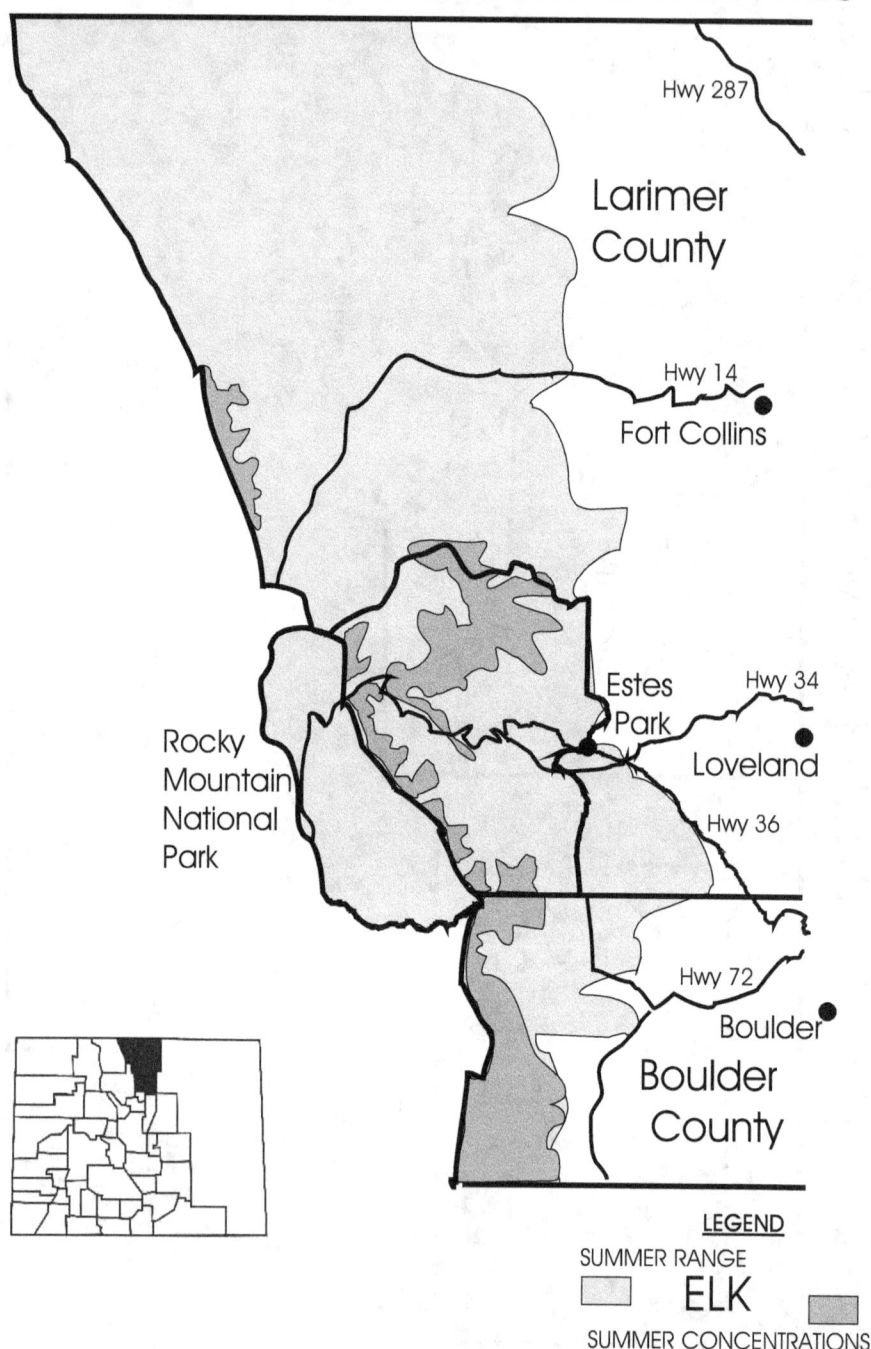

Hwy 287

Larimer County

Hwy 14

Fort Collins

Rocky Mountain National Park

Estes Park

Hwy 34

Loveland

Hwy 36

Hwy 72

Boulder

Boulder County

LEGEND

SUMMER RANGE

ELK

SUMMER CONCENTRATIONS

GILPIN, CLEAR CREEK, JEFFERSON, AND DOUGLAS COUNTIES

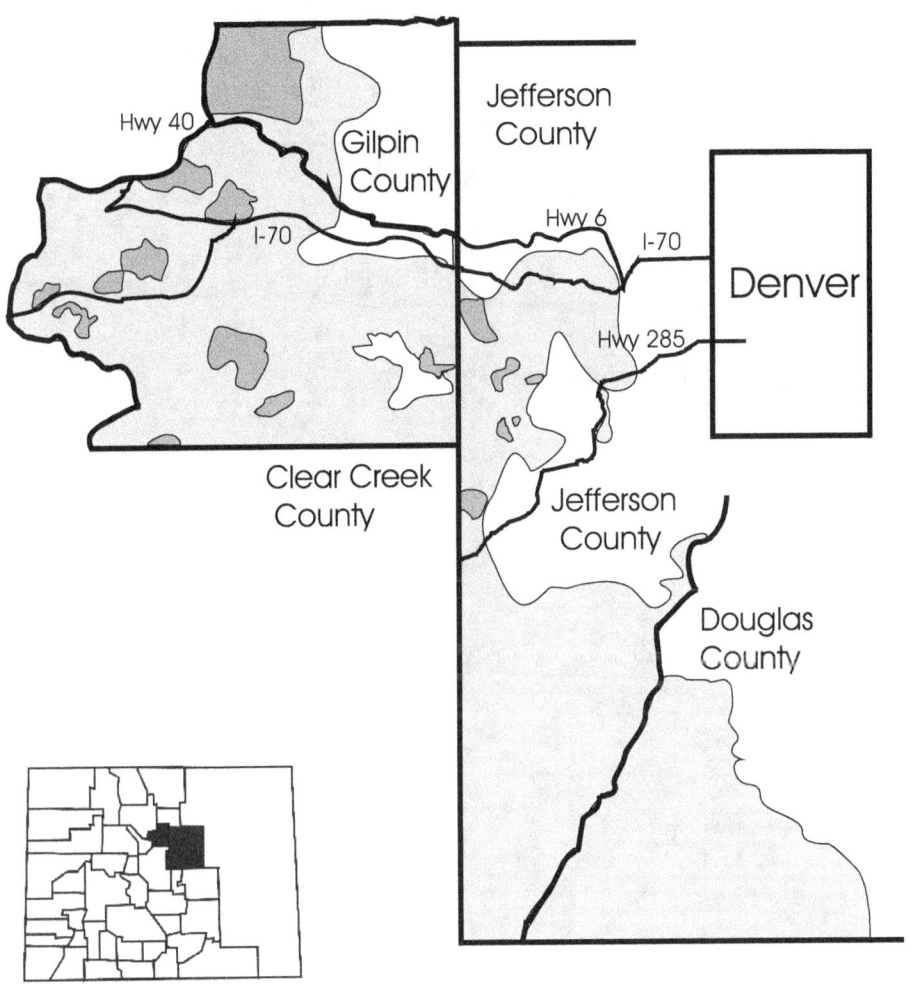

TELLER & EL PASO COUNTIES

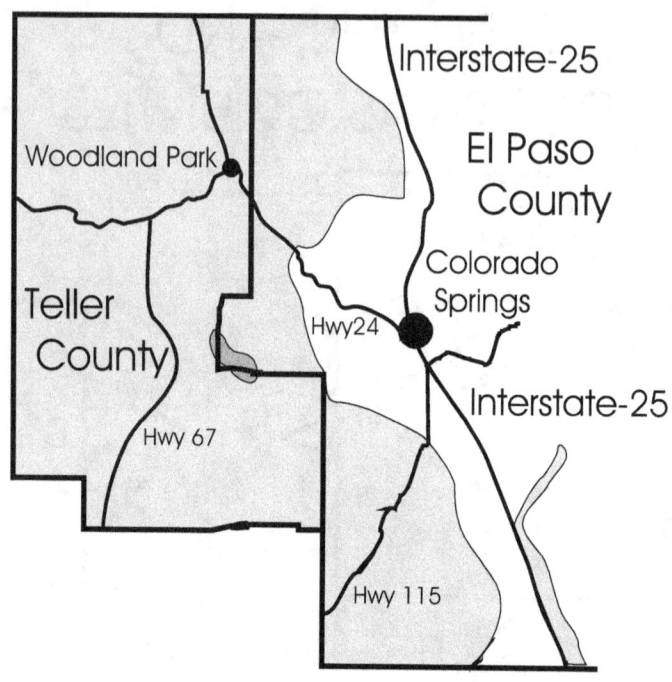

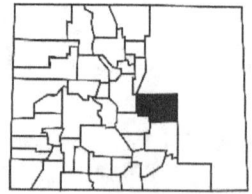

LEGEND

SUMMER RANGE

ELK

SUMMER CONCENTRATIONS

CUSTER & HUERFANO COUNTIES

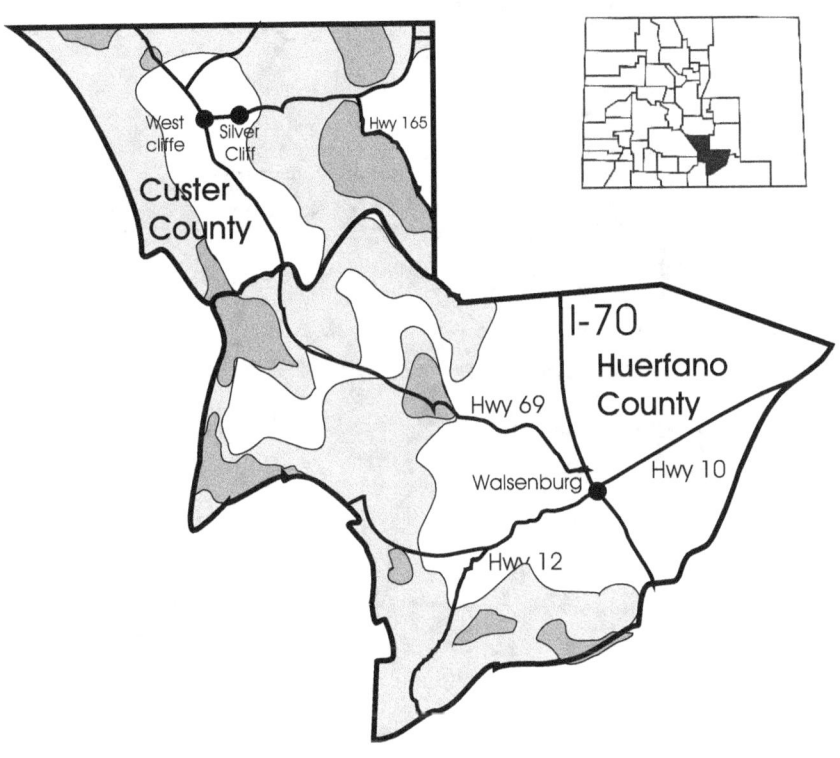

West
cliffe
Silver
Cliff
Hwy 165

Custer
County

I-70

Huerfano
County

Hwy 69

Walsenburg
Hwy 10

Hwy 12

PUEBLO COUNTY

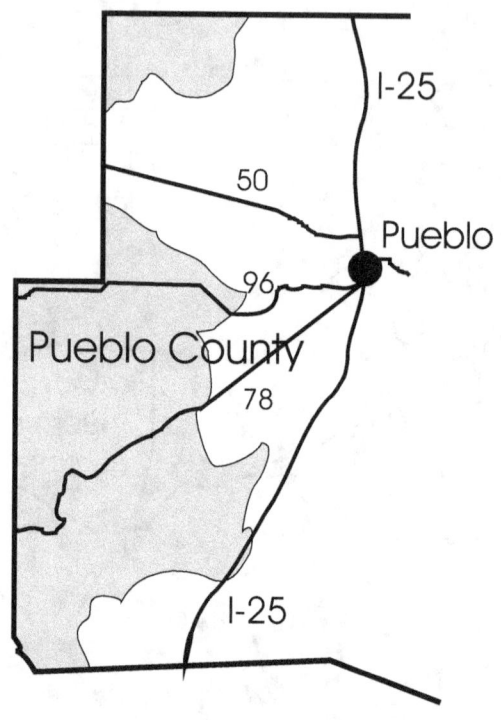

I-25

50

Pueblo

96

Pueblo County

78

I-25

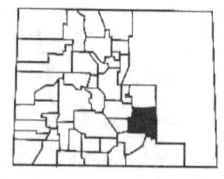

LAS ANIMAS COUNTY

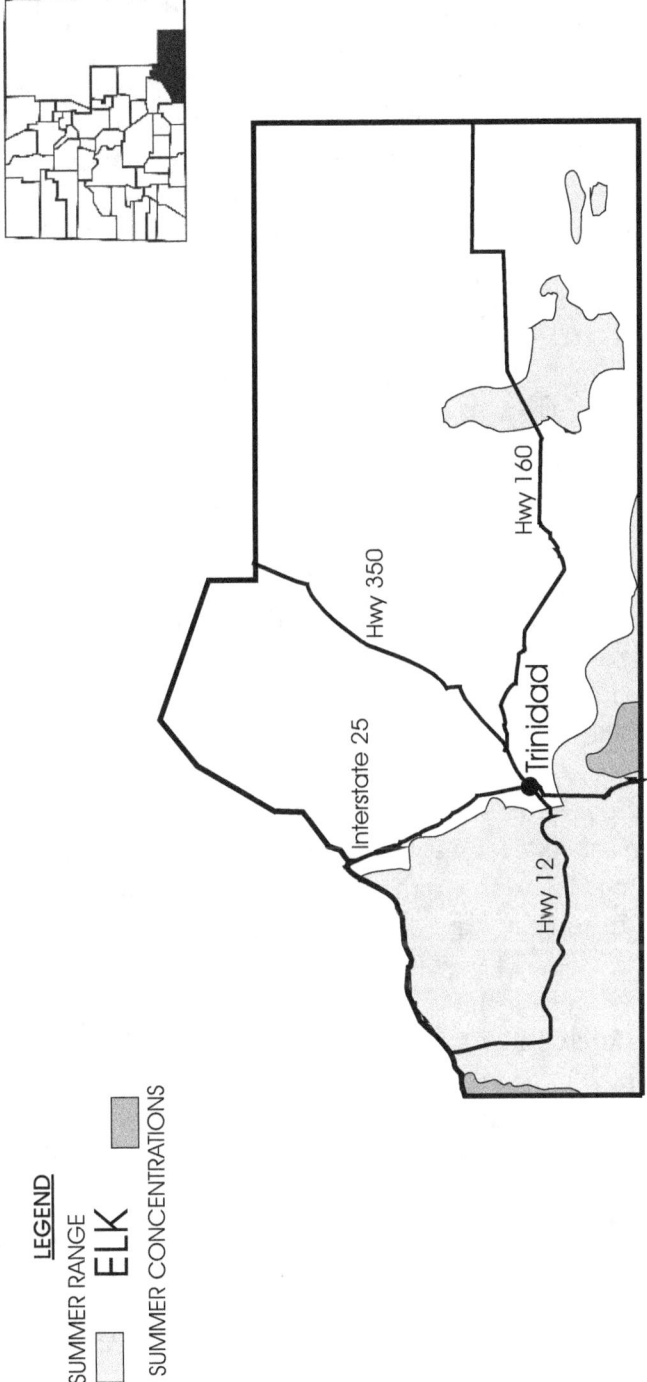

LEGEND

SUMMER RANGE

ELK

SUMMER CONCENTRATIONS

Interstate 25

Hwy 350

Hwy 160

Hwy 12

Trinidad

SOME MISCELLANEOUS AND IMPORTANT THOUGHTS

Hunting methods: I personally like the ambush or stand because when you are setting or standing still you have the advantage. I won't go into all the methods as those are adequately covered by many other authors. Just to mention a few for the "catalog". Stands, Still hunting, Drives, Spot and Stalk, just plain old casual walking, (I have run into more elk this way than any other method I can think of).

Success: I guarantee 0% success with this book. The rest is up to you.

Television programs: The hunting programs now available are of marvelous help. Not only are they entertaining but you can get great second hand experience which can put you years ahead of yourself.

Shooting: Shooting with a bow is adequately covered in other writings, etc. For shooting with a rifle, I'll repeat advice I was given by my uncle from Eagle, Colorado; "Shoot them until they go down. If they get up shoot them again!"

Giving them the sneak: Locally there are at least three concentrations of elk near me. One afternoon awhile back I wanted to learn something. There is a herd of maybe three hundred that winters on private land. You can drive past and park along the road and watch them in the hay fields. They stay there until May. I assume they go up to their calving grounds in June. One day my wife and I were watching them before church. I got a GPS fix on them. A few weeks later I took an afternoon to hike in from the opposite direction on public land. I had projected to an area where I assumed they might bed. Bingo! I walked right in on them. Elk ran all over the place after a cow up in the cedars gave the bark alarm.

What I'm saying here is that you might find it handy sometime to use this, around the end run tactic, to use football thinking to put you on elk. Terrain problems, like cliffs, etc. might dictate how you do this.

Best wishes in your quest and life.   Ed French